GUIDE

Building the Team. Setting the Direction.
Fulfilling the Mission.

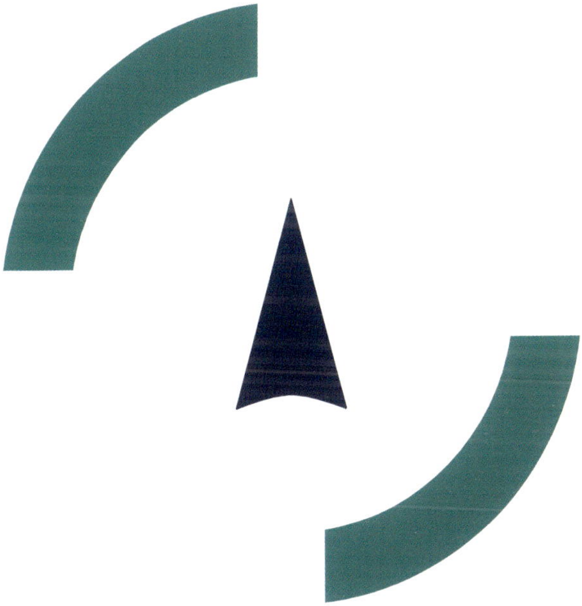

Jay R. Desko, Ph.D.
David A. Marks, D.Min.

Acknowledgments

The Center is a Christian consulting group whose highly trained team is passionate about advancing leadership and organizational health. We believe this resource about being an effective team leader will be helpful for you and your organization. We are providing this resource as an extension of our vision of advancing organizational health.

ISBN: 978-1-5323-6399-3

Design by Tiehl McRoberts

For more information about The Center, call 215-723-2325 or visit our website at www.centerconsulting.org.

THE CENTER
Guiding Organizations. Coaching Leaders.

Contents

Who Are We?

How Do We Change?

What You'll Learn

Most leaders, in moments of transparency, reveal both their passion for making a difference in the lives of their employees, customers, and communities as well as the challenges they experience along the journey – defining a vision, building a team, leading change, and implementing priorities. Exciting, yet challenging!

Welcome to leadership. You are not alone! Leadership is both energizing and hard work. And it is better done with a guide that can help you avoid the pain and see greater accomplishment. This book will guide you as you navigate the challenges common to leading. Whether you lead a business, nonprofit or church, you'll add new learning to your experience including:

- Understanding how others view your leadership
- Building successful teams
- Identifying what your organization needs to create and maintain momentum
- Recognizing when and why a plan will fail
- Making and implementing decisions
- Helping your team process change
- Implementing changes
- Managing roadblocks when they arise

Enjoy the journey as you aim to lead well!

“

Teamwork is the ability to work together toward a common vision... It is the fuel that allows common people to attain uncommon results.

ANDREW CARNEGIE

Section 1:
Who Are We?

Building a Team That Makes Good Happen

Understanding Your Natural Leadership Style

by Jay R. Desko, Ph.D.

6 Instinctive Approaches to Leading

There is now a book for almost everything "leadership." 7 Habits. 21 Laws. 5 Dysfunctions. 12 Disciplines. You get the point! There is much to be gained from practical books or articles on leadership. Yet, sometimes they take a long time to read and use many words to talk about leadership. This is also true when it comes to the topic of leadership types or styles. I make no claim to provide any new research on the topic of the differing approaches to leadership. However, in our years of consulting with nonprofits, businesses, and churches, we have observed six instinctive approaches to the way a leader leads. Most leaders are a combination of at least two of these approaches and, at times, may manifest characteristics from all of them.

Who Cares?

You may be wondering why you should care about the different leadership approaches. Well, the main reason is your approach to leadership can create health or dysfunction, attract or repel good employees, and lead to effective outcomes or organizational failure. The more you understand your approach to leading and the approach of those with whom you serve, the greater the likelihood you will improve team health and organizational effectiveness.

What Are the Six Approaches to Leadership?

Summary		
Leader Type	**Orientation**	**Primary Characteristic**
1. Driver	Action	Delivering results
2. Protector	Authority	Procedures in detail
3. Innovator	Vision	Creative idea generation
4. Expert	Knowledge	Professional expertise
5. Strategist	Planning	Plans for accomplishing goals
6. Relater	People	Relational glue

The Driver

DRIVER

Delivering results

Drivers are leaders who are energized by accomplishing a major goal. Supervisors, owners, and board members love Drivers when they are accomplishing the right initiatives, because without some level of decisiveness and execution, the organization will eventually flounder. However, if the Driver does not have the right expertise or relational skills, he may step on a few toes or crush a few feet!

Orientation:	Action
Greatest contribution:	Delivering results
Common challenge:	Moving too fast
What others say about you:	"He is too demanding."
What you say about yourself:	"I get things done."
What to do if you are a Driver:	Get the right information and strive to bring others with you.

The Protector

PROTECTOR

Procedures and detail

Protectors are wired to look at details and make sure every step in a process has been covered. They can add value because good processes can help to accomplish good outcomes. Without some level of decisiveness and innovation surrounding them, the Protector can easily begin to get bogged down. Because they often see the world in black and white and right and wrong, when process is not followed, they feel like the car is going off the road. This causes them to gravitate toward the use of command and control.

Orientation:	Authority
Greatest contribution:	Procedures and details
Common challenge:	Too slow
What others say about you:	"He micro-manages."
What you say about yourself:	"I protect the organization."
What to do if you are a Protector:	Focus on the big picture and strive for timely execution.

The Innovator

INNOVATOR

Creative idea generation

Innovators generate new ideas. These are the Steve Jobs (Apple), Mark Zuckerberg (Facebook), Jeff Bezos (Amazon), and Craig Groeschel (Life.Church) types. They see something that others have not yet seen or take an existing seed and grow it into a forest. Yet, without the right experts and planners, Innovators can experience expensive and damaging misfires. Or, they can simply wear out their team with too many new initiatives!

Orientation:	Vision
Greatest contribution:	Creative idea generation
Common challenge:	Too many ideas
What others say about you:	"She has no idea what it takes."
What you say about yourself:	"My ideas are innovative and are needed here."
What to do if you are an Innovator:	Focus on a few innovations and have others test those ideas.

The Expert

EXPERT

Professional expertise

Experts have specialized knowledge and experience. Over many years of study and practice, they have acquired knowledge that others may not have and can utilize that knowledge to avoid costly errors. But sometimes, their expertise can create blind spots that include arrogance ("I am smart and I know it") and the inability to learn from others since, after all, they are the smartest ones in the room!

Orientation:	Knowledge
Greatest contribution:	Professional expertise
Common challenge:	Too arrogant
What others say about you:	"He thinks he knows everything."
What you say about yourself:	"I know what I am talking about."
What to do if you are an Expert:	Don't think too highly of yourself, and don't be blinded by "knowledge."

The Strategist

STRATEGIST

Plans for accomplishing goals

Strategists are planners. They may not always be good at innovation and setting forth a destination, but they are energized by creating a map to reach the destination. Where an Innovator may lie awake at night overwhelmed just thinking about putting a plan together, Strategists lie awake at night because they are excited! Yet, if Strategists don't have any Innovators or Drivers around, they may get bogged down in details, and having the plan becomes the end rather than the means.

Orientation:	Planning
Greatest contribution:	Plans for accomplishing goals
Common challenge:	Too complex
What others say about you:	"He makes things too complicated."
What you say about yourself:	"I am great at ensuring goals are accomplished."
What to do if you are a Strategist:	Simple is better, and be reminded that a plan is a means and not an end.

The Relater

RELATER

Relational glue

Relaters love people-time! Whereas some of the other leadership styles may be drained by people, the Relater's tank is filled by time with people. They are often fun, positive, and add good chemistry to a team. However, if Relaters don't have a Driver or Strategist around, they may spend too much time talking and schmoozing and not actually get anything done! The strength of people skills can be over-taken by the perception of "all talk, no action."

Orientation:	People
Greatest contribution:	Relational glue
Common challenge:	Too little action
What others say about you:	"She spends too much time schmoozing."
What you say about yourself:	"Leaders need to be more people-oriented... like me."
What to do if you are a Relater:	Be reminded that talk is not action – there is also work to be done.

What Next?

Our approach to leadership matters. It affects those around us as well as the long-term health and effectiveness of our organizations. There is not one "correct" approach. We are unique individuals; each approach has important elements and no one approach contains all that is needed. Leaders often make two common mistakes:

1. Trying to be something they were not created to be
2. Doing too much reading and learning and not enough changing

Andrew Jackson said, "Take time to deliberate; but when the time for action arrives, stop thinking and go in." As you take time to consider your approach to leadership and the leadership of those around you, I encourage you to consider the following action steps:

1. **Be reminded.** The Bible says we are both wonderfully made (Psalm 139) and, sadly, also corrupt (Jeremiah 17). As leaders, none of us are perfect in our attitudes, skills or practice.

2. **Know yourself.** Know your leadership style, strengths, and blind spots. You cannot manage what you do not know.

3. **Team up.** Surround yourself with the right people. You need those who compliment your style by providing what you are missing.

4. **Seek cultural fit.** Work in positions and places where your style is a fit for the culture.

5. **Don't make excuses.** Don't use your leadership style as an excuse for bad behavior or incompetence!

How Healthy Is Your Leadership?

by Jay R. Desko, Ph.D.

Lies Leaders Believe

"Keep lies far from me." –Proverbs 30:8

It's easy to get caught up in the power of a leadership position. But it's important to maintain a truthful view of yourself and to not become inflated. Look out for these ten lies that leaders often believe.

1. I am irreplaceable!

Most leaders believe they are irreplaceable – but in reality, 30 days after they are dead, the organization will be running just fine.

2. Those around me are telling me the truth!

Note to self – they are not. Most team members lower the volume of what they feel when sharing with you.

3. My worth is determined by my success!

Hard to resist this one, but eventually you will age out or be pushed out of your leadership role. God determines your worth; your position and success don't.

4. I know better than everyone else – that's why I am the boss!

The often heard phrase still stands – none of us is as smart as all of us.

5. My success of the past guarantees my success in the present!

As Marshall Goldsmith said, "What got you here won't get you there." Past successes have a short shelf life.

6. I could see my blind spots if I had any!

Here is a profound note – you do have them, and so do I. This is why the Apostle Paul reminds us in Romans 12:3 to look at ourselves with "sober judgment."

7. I am as good as everyone tells me I am!

Nope. Not really. You may be talented, and you may be well liked, but when you are in a leadership role, people have a habit of telling you what you want to hear.

8. If everyone doesn't like me, something is wrong!

In reality, something is very wrong if everyone does like you. Leadership isn't about being liked; it's about doing the right thing. In Luke 6:26, Jesus reminds us, "Woe to you when everyone speaks well of you."

9. I am entitled to special treatment – after all, I am the leader!

You may be the leader, and you may be worthy of greater benefits because of your talents, but entitlement can take you down a road of more, more, more . . . a road with no end.

10. Power can corrupt others, but not me!

In reality, the more power you acquire, the more you tend to become selfish and abusive. Dacher Keltner provides four antidotes: graciousness, empathy, gratitude, and generosity.

Building Effective Teams

by Jay R. Desko, Ph.D.

Why Teams?

Have you ever noticed how most titles for organizational leadership are singular – referring to only one person? For example, businesses often mention the president of the company. Nonprofits commonly use executive director when describing their top person. Churches most often use senior pastor. Sports teams have a general manager. These all refer to just one person. This is not necessarily a problem since it has been historically common to have one person defined as a leader and it can certainly make organizational life more uniform and efficient. However, regardless of whether you have one person at the top or you have a team of people who share leadership, today's complexity necessitates plurality. In other words, if you want to succeed, you will definitely need a team of skilled people who are working together. One talented leader is no longer sufficient.

There is an often quoted passage from the Old Testament book Ecclesiastes that sheds light on the practical benefit of teamwork and interdependency.

> "Two are better than one, because they have a good return for their labor: If either of them falls down, one can help the other up. But pity anyone who falls and has no one to help them up. Also, if two lie down together, they will keep warm. But how can one keep warm alone? Though one may be overpowered, two can defend themselves. A cord of three strands is not quickly broken." –Ecclesiastes 4:9-12

Why team up? As explained in Ecclesiastes, some of the benefits include:

1. Higher performance
2. Better decisions
3. Greater support for one another
4. Better quality of life

By intentionally creating high functioning teams, your organization can experience these benefits.

When Teams Can Be a Hindrance

While we believe effective teaming is a vital part of a successful organization, there are times when teams can be more of a hindrance than a help. Here are a few examples:

Groupthink. Groupthink happens when a group's interactions and dynamics bring about either conformity or fear of conflict and punishment which can result in perceived agreement rather than actual agreement. The outcome is often that the team's decision becomes less desirable than the individual's decision.

Weak members. A team that has a weak member is like a chain that has a weak link. It can weaken the performance of the whole team and hold back the higher performing members. In addition, if this goes on too long, your highest performing members will eventually look for a new team!

Poor use of time. Teams are not the best at solving simple problems. In fact, it can become expensive if you have a lot of staff hours being invested into a simple problem. It can also be frustrating to team members since they see the inefficiency of it.

Common Leadership Structures

While we believe that teaming up is a vital part of building a highly effective and healthy organization, today's organizational leadership structures utilize teams to differing levels.

1. The Positional Authority Model

In this model, one leader is considered the top person based upon his or her position or title. This is the most common model especially among more traditional and established organizations.

> **Team Factor:** Low dependence on team
>
> **Greatest Challenges:** The complex nature of organizational leadership today makes it increasingly difficult for the autocratic, singular leader to have all the skills necessary to successfully lead an organization into the future. In addition, highly skilled staff, especially

those who are younger, are not as likely to desire to be told what to do but would rather work collaboratively toward a shared vision and future.

2. The Charismatic Leader Model

In this model, one highly influential and inspirational person is the shaping influence in setting direction and leading the organization. This is especially common in new or fast-growing organizations with influential founders.

Team Factor: Low dependence on team

Greatest Challenges: There are a limited number of highly skilled charismatic leaders from which to choose. Such gifted leaders can choose from the best, largest, and highest paying opportunities, making it difficult for the average organization to recruit one of them. And, should such a leader become narcissistic, there can be serious consequences.

3. Coach/Team Model

In this model, a point leader has authority over what is happening but generally works collaboratively with his or her team to accomplish the vision.

Team Factor: Moderate dependence on team

Greatest Challenges: While this model can result in better collaboration, the top leader (coach) does not have to follow the advice of the team and the team does not have authority to prevent or correct poor decisions made by the leader.

4. The Shared Authority Model

This model has anywhere from two to four leaders who have equal authority and work collaboratively to develop vision and direction as well as oversee staff in the departments for which they are responsible.

> **Team Factor:** High dependence on team
>
> **Greatest Challenges:** Requires high levels of trust and fit. No one member can strongly desire to be the "alpha" or top leader. In addition, decision-making can be slow and/or confusing.

Remember, there are no perfect leadership models. Most models can succeed or fail depending on the skills, attitude and relational health of the individuals filling the position(s).

6 Characteristics of High Performing Teams

Every effective leadership team needs the right elements to be successful. The following list includes the top six characteristics of high performing teams.

SHARE **VISION**

1. Share Vision

How would you like to get on a plane and have everyone advocating for going to different locations? The result would be chaos and frustration! A high performing team always has a shared vision and shared priorities. While they may not agree on every nuance, this shared vision unifies them and provides focus for their energy.

"Teamwork is the ability to work together toward a common vision; the ability to direct individual accomplishments toward organizational objectives. It is the fuel that allows common people to attain uncommon results." –Andrew Carnegie

LOVE **WORK**

2. Love Work

If you love what you do and why you do it, you will reflect a passion for it.

I believe that leaders and team members would do better to assess passion for the work rather than just count hours on the job. We find that almost all of the leaders we have worked with who are successful in what they are doing manifest an energy or passion for it. In other words, they love what they do! Not every part of it and not every moment, but if you absolutely love 75% or more of what you do, you will feel less stress, complain less about your job, and wake up energized to get to it. Far too many leaders are more passionate about their hobbies than the organization's vision. Team members who love their work add great value.

"The two most important days in your life are the day you are born and the day you find out why."
–Mark Twain

WORK **HARD**

3. Work Hard

Pick an expert in any field and you will find they have invested extraordinary hours of study and practice. Athlete. Surgeon. Musician. If they are world class, they have invested well over 10,000 hours of practice. This is how leaders feel when they work hard at something for which they are passionate. If someone is complaining about the work, it sometimes means:

- He may be working at something he does not love
- His tank is being drained by personal issues in his life
- He has a low level of endurance or stamina

Remember, one team member who does not work hard can negatively impact the morale and performance of the whole team.

"It's all hard work. Nothing comes easy. But I have a lot of fun!" –Rupert Murdoch, media mogul

STAY **SHARP**

4. Stay Sharp

In creating a high performing team, you need a diversity of skills and each team member's commitment to continually improve those skills. Your value to the team is influenced by how well you stay on top of your professional skills. When you allow them to slip, your value to the team is diminished and you hinder the impact of the organization. Research has shown that experts, or those who are the best of the best, are four times as productive as an average member of the team.

There is nothing normal or natural about expertise. It requires purposeful effort, which is another phrase for hard work! You know you have it when you see someone consistently perform far above those around him/her.

COMMUNICATE **OFTEN**

5. Communicate Often

I have never once heard a leader or team be accused of over-communicating. Not once! We may feel we have shared the right information in the right volume, but we often forget that people are overwhelmed with messages and most people really are not very good listeners! The same is often true on leadership teams. Research at MIT's Human Dynamics Lab found that high performing team members balance the amount they talk and listen.

Regardless of using email, social media, or face-to-face communication, it takes time to talk. But it is time well worth it since such communication helps build and maintain shared understanding and trust. People often ask, "How can a team make a decision?" The answer is rather simple: collaboratively. High performing leadership teams know how to fight well since passion and personality will sometimes lead to disagreement. Such disagreements, when taking place upon a foundation of relationship, respect and trust, are very beneficial for the overall effectiveness of the team.

"Two monologues do not make a dialogue." –Jeff Daly

RELATE **WELL**

6. Relate Well

The foundation for any strong relationship is trust and respect, and it is critical that a team relates well to one another. Respect and trust are formed by consistently demonstrating character and competency. In other words, trust is the reliance or confidence that other members of the team will generally meet the expectations we have of them. The more we successfully meet these expectations, the more others will perceive us through the filter of "this is a trustworthy person." Distrust develops when we fail to live up to the expectations others have of us. As distrust becomes embedded, it then becomes a filter through which many other actions or behaviors are judged. It takes time to form deep trust and respect. It requires intentional effort to create trust, and it requires almost no effort to lose it!

When selecting a high performing leadership team, you not only must determine how capable each individual is, but also how effective he/she will be with the collective team. An effective leadership team requires unity of vision and also necessitates a level of differentiation; each person brings a different set of skills and perspectives that work together. But it is also the job of each team member to help set the tone of unity by manifesting good emotional and relational skills. The following quote illustrates the importance of unity and emotional intelligence in team function:

> "In the last few decades, much research has proven the superiority of group decision-making over that of even the brightest individual in the group. There is one exception to this rule. If the group lacks harmony or the ability to cooperate, decision-making quality and speed suffer. Research at Cambridge University found that even groups comprising brilliant individuals will make bad decisions if the group disintegrates into bickering, interpersonal rivalry, or power plays. In short, groups are smarter than individuals only when they exhibit the qualities of emotional intelligence. Everyone in the group contributes to the overall level of emotional intelligence, but the leader holds special sway in this regard. Emotions are contagious and it's natural for people to pay attention to the leader's feelings and behavior. So, very often it is the group leader who sets the tone and helps to create the group's emotional reality – how it feels to be a part of the team. A leader skilled in collaboration can keep resonance high and thus ensure that the group's decisions will be worth the effort of meeting. Such leaders know how to balance a team's focus on the task at hand with attention to the relationships among the team members. They naturally create a friendly, cooperative climate in the room, a climate that fosters a positive outlook on the future."

–Daniel Goleman, Richard E. Boyatzis, and Annie McKee, *Primal Leadership: Learning to Lead with Emotional Intelligence*, 2013

Markers of Team Cohesion

Teaming up with the right people focused on the right vision can produce life-changing outcomes and be a whole lot of fun along the journey. When a team is performing at its best, it has resonance. The markers of team cohesion include:

- Trust and confidence
- Shared vision
- Joy, fun and celebration
- True sense of "we"
- Avoidance of triangulation
- Minimal undiscussed issues
- Minimal conflict and tension
- Minimal relational avoidance

Team cohesion both feels good to the team members and produces good results. But every team will eventually have to face some challenges. The Center consultants are experts at helping good teams become even better as well as helping struggling teams diagnose and resolve challenges. If we can help you in your effort to team up, please contact us!

How Healthy Is Your Team Performance?

1 2 3 4 5 6 7 8 9 10

SHARE VISION: Team members possess a shared vision & shared priorities

1 2 3 4 5 6 7 8 9 10

LOVE WORK: Team members display passion & energy for their work

1 2 3 4 5 6 7 8 9 10

WORK HARD: Team members diligently invest energy & time into their work

1 2 3 4 5 6 7 8 9 10

STAY SHARP: Team members continually work to enhance their skills

1 2 3 4 5 6 7 8 9 10

COMMUNICATE OFTEN: Team members balance the amount they talk & listen

1 2 3 4 5 6 7 8 9 10

RELATE WELL: Team members trust & respect one another

Your Score:

_____ Share Vision
_____ Love Work
_____ Work Hard
_____ Stay Sharp
_____ Communicate Often
_____ Relate Well

_____ **Your Total**

39 or below: Likelihood of lower team performance

40-49: Likelihood of moderate team performance

50-60: Likelihood of higher team performance

Shaping Culture

by Jay R. Desko, Ph.D.

4 Ways to Shape Your Organization's Culture

"Corporate." "Casual." "Friendly." "Excellent." "Ruthless." Ever hear these words when someone was describing where he/she works? These are a sampling of cultural descriptors. Every organization, department, board, and even family has a culture – a unique climate created by the values and beliefs of either a founder or leader and maintained by the expectations and behaviors of the leader and members. The following are four ways you can shape the culture of your team or organization.

1. Understanding

Culture is not so easy to understand, especially for those who are closest to it. To see culture more accurately, you need to seek input from both those within it as well as those who are more removed from it. Experienced consultants can utilize tools such as interviews, observation, and surveys to help you see your culture more accurately.

2. Staffing

Every time someone is added to a team, board or organization, the culture will change. Make sure you add those who can contribute to the culture you desire. If you value collaboration and hire an autocrat, you will have a culture clash. Likewise, if you want high performance but hire a low energy member, the result may be frustration.

3. Modeling

What leaders say and do will shape the culture for good or bad. In other words, the leader(s) shapes the culture by embedding his/her values. These include the leader's mood, words, actions and inactions. Then the culture shapes everyone else. Leaders need to understand this, own this, and make sure others can speak truth to them without the fear of losing their heads!

4. Responding

Crises have a powerful impact on our culture. These can be crises outside the organization such as the 9/11 attack or the introduction of a new game-changing technology, or they can be a crisis inside the organization such as a moral failure. Any of these can result in deep change. While we cannot always prevent a crisis from happening, we can control how we manage our response.

Investing in Younger Leaders

by Jay R. Desko, Ph.D.

Top 7 Ways to Invest in a Younger Leader

I had many people invest in me when I was a young leader, but one person in particular had the greatest influence in shaping who I am even to this day. Here are 7 practical ways he invested in me. Use these to invest in the younger leaders in your life!

1. Pick carefully

Select someone in whom you see high potential and a teachable attitude as well as someone who will be a good fit with you.

2. Take risks

Allow the young leader to actually lead by entrusting him/her with valued opportunities.

3. Eat!

Just kidding! Only partly. Spend time with the young leader beyond just work. Meals are a great starting place.

4. Share your credibility

Young leaders need you to loan some of your hard-earned credibility chips until they can earn their own.

5. Be natural

Don't try to make this robotic or programmatic. It's the relationship that counts the most!

6. Be transparent

Let them know not only about your successes but also about how you failed and navigated those failures.

7. Learn from them

Young leaders not only have much to learn, but they also have much to share with us. Take advantage of their perspectives, knowledge and experiences.

7 WAYS TO INVEST IN A YOUNGER LEADER

01 Pick carefully

02 Take risks

03 Eat!

04 Share your credibility

05 Be natural

06 Be transparent

07 Learn from them

Building Effective Boards

by Jay R. Desko, Ph.D.

Why Should I Care?

There are over 15 million leaders serving on the boards of an estimated 1.5 million nonprofit organizations and over 330,000 churches in the United States with a combined budget of over $800,000 billion dollars! And the combined societal impact of these nonprofits is beyond comprehension as they address vital issues such as medical research, health care, homelessness, disabilities, aging, feeding the hungry, and foster care, just to name a few. The effectiveness of a nonprofit board can make or break the success of its mission. The principles that are essential to leading a nonprofit can also add great value to other enterprises including your own.

If boards are so important, why do we often hear comments such as...

“I dread going to another board meeting.” –Board Member

“My board is so frustrating; I am thinking about moving on.” –Executive Director

"I feel like our board is nothing but a rubber stamp for the CEO." –Board Member

"Some of our board members are just not willing to change." –Board Chair

"I am getting off this board at the first opportunity." –Board Member

As consultants, we are often asked to help with staff and board roles, conflict, and effectiveness. While boards were created to serve the mission, the result is sometimes more harm than help, conflict rather than collaboration, and policing rather than partnering. Nonprofit boards need to start with this foundational principle:

The board is not the mission but rather exists to serve the mission.

In other words, board policies and by-laws are not the end but rather a means to the end – to the mission and vision of the organization. This chapter will help boards better understand emerging trends that are likely affecting them as well as discuss board purpose, roles, and effective board leadership. Since all types of organizations could benefit from building a healthier board, the term "director" will be used synonymously in place of the terms Executive Director, CEO and Senior Pastor.

Current Trends & Observations

1. Christian nonprofit boards, especially churches, are distinct from other nonprofit boards because they must fulfill both legal and spiritual responsibilities and because the board members are often the recipients of the services offered by the organizations they govern. At times, this can create awkwardness at best and perceived conflict of interest at worst since the board members can sometimes forget which hat they are wearing: board hat or participant hat. To be effective, you must know which hat you are wearing (personal or board) and be constantly reminded that your goals and needs are subordinate to the goals and needs of the organization.

2. Boards are still expected to fulfill their fiduciary/accountability responsibilities though these responsibilities may not require significant time and may not be very challenging. This is true when an organization is in a time of steady operations without major changes inside or outside of the organization. It is also especially true as an organization grows and hires more professional staff to fulfill positions which skilled board member volunteers once filled. Since board members have been acculturated into these roles, frustration and conflict with staff often results.

3. The shortage of younger leaders with the right skills and experience needed by boards combined with having 1.5 million 501(c)(3) organizations can result in the decreasing ability to attract and retain highly

skilled thinkers and leaders. In other words, there may be more nonprofits in need of skilled board members than there are board members to recruit; there are not enough to go around! This sometimes results in boards accepting members who are not adequately qualified or are not a good fit. Some refer to this as the "If They Can Fog a Mirror Test," a metaphor for, "If they have a heartbeat, they are good enough."

4. It used to be that boards seldom experienced change. They were steady and predictable, and they functioned the same way year after year. However, the emergence of a slow but powerful tsunami including cultural, demographic, worldview and technological shifts, will significantly alter the nature of board leadership for most nonprofits including social services, schools, camps, churches and missions. Boards will need to grow smaller, eliminate "board member for life" by ensuring rotation, adjust the types of members they recruit based upon what the organization is facing, and meet less frequently but as often as needed to fulfill their role.

Be Flexible

Mention "board" to many leaders today, and the first thoughts are often negative, using words like – slow, bureaucratic, boring, sluggish to change, controlling and inflexible. While we have found this to be untrue with many of the organizations we have served, it is important to remind boards in this new environment of accelerated change and uncertainty that flexibility is essential.

This flexibility is first and foremost an attitude. Flexibility will provide greater adaptability when it comes time for making needed changes including board size, frequency of meetings, and new program initiatives. It is also especially applicable to the issue of control. As consultants, we have found that the top sources of organizational conflict are control, vision/direction, and leadership changes. Excessive control may grow out of distrust and fear, resulting in slow decisions and decreasing creativity. Excessive decentralization may grow out of an unwillingness to submit to others, and it may lead to chaos and poor decisions.

HIGHLY CENTRALIZED	HIGHLY DECENTRALIZED
Slow decision making	Fast decision making
Low creativity	High creativity
Positional power	Relational power
Structure & control	Ambiguity & chaos
Higher accountability	Lower accountability
Rigid	Flexible
Slow to adapt & change	Quick to adapt & change
Centralized power & decisions	Dispersed power & decisions
Few leaders	Many leaders
Leaders direct & control	Leaders cultivate & encourage
High risk when leader transitions	Low risk when leader transitions

Set Up Your Board

There are different types of boards for different purposes and seasons of an organization's life stage. Boards must select the type they need to be in order to build an effective board to meet their objective.

Types of Boards

- **Policy Governance (Carver) Model** - Board sets mission and policy, allowing the director to utilize the means. This is often referred to as "Staff Led/Board Governed."

- **Operations Model** - Board participates in functional areas deciding, and perhaps implementing, the decisions.

- **Representative Model** - Board members represent different areas of the organization.

- **Funding/Symbolic Model** - Board is selected primarily for name recognition and/or giving potential.

- **Advisory/Support Model** - Board serves to advise the director, providing guidance in areas such as law, finance, HR, etc.

- **Strategic Leadership Model** - Board works collaboratively with the director(s) to define future direction, priorities and sometimes strategy.

Understand the Roles & Expectations

An agreement on expectations and roles is essential for building trust and high performance as well as keeping conflict and frustration to a minimum. Three particularly common areas of conflict and confusion between a director and a board are spending authority, hiring/supervision/firing authority, and programming changes. As a board, it may be beneficial to review and discuss the "Roles and Expectations" chart on the next page. Where is there agreement? Where are you doing well or not so well?

When expectations are not agreed upon or clear, leadership erosion takes place with sometimes devastating consequences. This cycle and the contributing factors are noted in the graphic below. Expectation agreement and management is truly mission-critical!

THE CYCLE OF LEADERSHIP EROSION

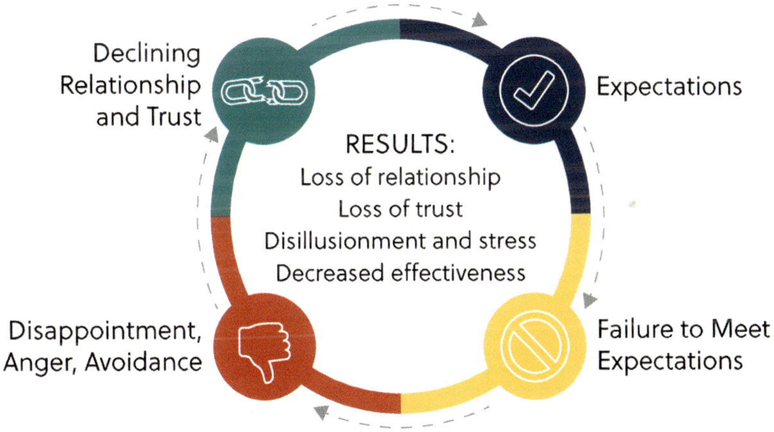

CONTRIBUTING FACTORS INCLUDE:

Insufficient relational connection
Insufficient fit and chemistry
Inability to manage conflict effectively
Inadequate early intervention
Absence of a unifying vision
Lack of courage to act

Roles and Expectations

CEO/ Director	Attitude	• Manifest Christ-like attitude and integrity personally and professionally
	Staff	• Recruit, evaluate, and supervise staff • Ensure the staff operates within the laws, policies, and mission of the organization
	Organization	• Collaboratively develop vision and strategic plan • Protect and accomplish the mission • Ensure creation and oversight of annual budget
	Board	• Show respect to the board • Practice the "no surprise rule" with chair & board
Chair	Attitude	• Manifest Christ-like attitude and integrity personally and professionally
	Director	• Work collaboratively with the director to create meeting agendas • Practice the "no surprise rule" with the director
	Board	• Lead board meetings by managing the conversation, dynamics, time, and agenda • In collaboration with the director, organize the board to accomplish its work • Regularly lead the board through evaluation of its health and effectiveness
Executive Team	Attitude	• Manifest Christ-like attitude and integrity personally and professionally
	Director	• Conduct the director evaluation • Practice the "no surprise rule" with the director • Set compensation for the director
	Board	• Recruit and nominate new board members for approval
Board	Attitude	• Manifest Christ-like attitude and integrity personally and professionally
	Director	• Hire and provide accountability to the director • Protect the director • Practice the "no surprise rule" with the director
	Organization	• Be a positive ambassador for the organization • Set and protect the mission • Test and approve vision and strategic plan • Approve major policies & oversee fiscal health • Financially support the organization • Ensure the overall health of the organization

Know the Signs of Board Health & Dysfunction

When you go to the doctor or the Emergency Room, one of the first things they do is take your vital signs. These signs are called "vital" for a reason. When any one of the vital signs, like blood pressure or temperature, is far out of the acceptable range, you know you have a problem that needs to be addressed immediately. The same is true for boards; you need to regularly check the vital signs.

HEALTHY BOARDS vs. UNHEALTHY BOARDS

The following are vital signs related to healthy and unhealthy boards. Use these charts for both discussion and evaluation of your board's health.

Healthy Boards

+ Clear expectations for the board and the director
+ Relentless pursuit of relationship among the board and with the director
+ Frequent and transparent communication
+ High level of trust and confidence with one another
+ Compelling and unifying vision and strategy
+ Agreed upon expectations
+ Few unhealthy "surprises"
+ Flexibility and forgiveness
+ Periodic board evaluation

Unhealthy Boards

- Members withholding essential questions
- Difficulty in recruiting competent members
- Avoidance of difficult discussions
- Surprising decisions, actions, or words
- Frequent attrition, poor attendance, infrequent giving
- Unexpected resignations of board members or executive staff
- Regular turnover of the director
- Minimal vulnerability in sharing about personal lives
- Key discussions often taking place outside the board

Wisely Recruit Board Members

Recruiting and selecting board members must be done with great wisdom. One bad board member can result in a lot of conflict, damage and frustration. It is hard to find board members these days, but it is even harder to remove a bad one! New board members need to:

1. Have a good reputation
2. Possess the right skills to address the present needs of the organization
3. Be committed to the mission and vision
4. Have a reasonable level of emotional and relational health
5. Have the time needed to participate

In addition, good boards often need a blend of the following unique characteristics:

- **Experts** – Known for possessing specialized knowledge relevant to the organization. They provide the expertise needed for making sound decisions.
- **Catalysts** – Known for being innovative, future oriented, and big picture thinkers. They move an organization beyond its present state.
- **Relaters** – Known for encouragement, humor, and enthusiasm. They add joy to teams and meetings.
- **Testers** – Known for candor, assertiveness, and testing assumptions through questioning. They help guard against major mistakes.

Practice Good Communication & Decision-Making

In their article "The Passive-Aggressive Organization" published in *Harvard Business Review* in 2005, Gary L. Neilson, Bruce A. Pasternack, and Karen E. Van Nuys make this unfortunate but accurate statement about leadership decision-making:

> "Clarifying and articulating decision rights is often the first order of business in fixing a passive-aggressive organization where decisions have been made, unmade, overturned, and second-guessed so many times that no one really knows who truly decides what any more."

The graphic below demonstrates the range of approaches to board-staff roles.

BOARD-STAFF CONTINUUM

BOARD LEADS DIRECTOR IMPLEMENTS

- Attracts average staff
- Ministry dependent upon the board
- Common in smaller organizations

DIRECTOR LEADS BOARD GOVERNS

- Requires skilled board and staff
- Necessitates mutual trust
- Greater accountability
- Common in growing organizations
- Decisions take longer

DIRECTOR LEADS BOARD ADVISES

- Often hierarchical and high control
- Common with founders
- Often lacks accountability
- Decisions made more quickly

Establishing good patterns of communication and decision-making is important for efficient and effective board leadership. When communicating with the director, it is helpful to know what is expected. For example, when the director brings an item to the board, both he and the board chair should know in advance if:

- This is only for **information** for the board – the decision resides with the director.
- This is for **input** from the board – but the decision resides with the director.
- This is for **approval** – the board has the authority to decide.

If intentions are unclear, confusion and conflict can result easily and quickly. For example, if a director brings something to the board for only discussion or input and the board believes their input will be implemented, the board may feel the director did not listen. If the board shares some ideas with the director that they expect to be implemented, the director may feel these were merely suggestions, not mandates. Clarity is easier on the front end in comparison to hurt feelings and distrust later on.

Structure Carefully

Four key areas of board structure relate to size, terms, meetings and executive sessions.

Board Size

Board size should be driven by the unique needs and life stage of the organization. Smaller is better (5-9). Larger boards make it difficult to recruit and fill vacancies, and they increase the complexity of scheduling and decision-making.

Board Terms

Term length plays an important role by ensuring continuity through change processes while providing opportunity for fresh ideas and energy. If terms are too long, some may decline service. If they are too short, the likelihood of disruption to major decisions and change initiatives increases.

Frequency of Meetings

Boards need to meet as often as necessary to fulfill their role. Meeting too often will waste time and meeting too infrequently will allow possibilities for oversight. The season of life will determine the frequency. Many boards meet too often, resulting in a lack of meaningful discussion and work. In addition, meeting too often can result in creating items for discussion that are not needed except to build time into the meeting agenda.

Executive Sessions

Executive sessions are when the board meets without the presence of the director. Such meetings can be valuable but also problematic if not managed wisely. Some directors can become nervous or insecure when these meetings take place. Some board members can misuse these meetings which can lead to unintended conflict and distrust. Executive sessions are primarily for the purpose of evaluating the director or addressing a charge against him or her. Beyond these general purposes, such sessions should be scheduled with care. In addition, it is wise for the board chair to provide an update to the director regarding what was discussed and the related outcomes.

Keep the Organization Disciplined & Focused

It is easy for nonprofit organizations to lose their focus. Chasing donor money, implementing too many "good ideas," and failing to embed and preserve a biblical worldview often leads to slow erosion. It is not uncommon for a nonprofit to start a new program simply because a donor said he/she would help fund it. However, this program will need to be continually funded long into the future unless its economic engine produces self-sustaining revenue. This often results in the director and staff having to run faster on the fundraising treadmill. A board must help a nonprofit stay focused by asking strategic questions. Most nonprofit organizations have a compelling mission, but they often lack differentiation from other organizations and seldom have a clear strategy and supporting programs. In her 2004 *Harvard Business Review* article titled "Lofty Missions, Down-to-Earth Plans," V. Kasturi Rangan warns that because nonprofits have such compelling and lofty missions, it is easy to drift into valuable yet undisciplined addition of programs. The author encourages boards to especially focus on asking strategic questions such as:

- What is the strategy?
- Does the organization have a coherent model to execute the strategy?
- How effective are our programs?
- How efficiently are they executed?

- Which programs should we drop?
- Which should we seek to add?

Hire Wisely & Evaluate Appropriately

One hiring mistake can cost an average small/modestly sized nonprofit $150,000-$250,000, not including damaged relationships, reputations and morale. Contributing factors to a hiring mistake include:

- Unclear expectations between the board and the director
- Inadequate relational/emotional management skills of the director
- Poor search process and inexperience in hiring a nonprofit director
- Groupthink that results in a failure to raise concerns regarding the candidates
- Inadequate test for fit with the organizational and board culture

Know who you are, what you want, and who you are hiring BEFORE you hire! It is wise to utilize the guidance of professionals in thinking through and managing your hiring process.

Additionally, it is shocking how often we hear of a board that hired a director but then never provided regular feedback or evaluation. It's important to regularly provide clear and agreed upon expectations and then feedback regarding these expectations. This should be an ongoing process and also formally done by the chair or an executive committee of the board each year. It is also valuable to periodically conduct a 360° assessment for the director. It is best to have this facilitated by a third party who will review the feedback with the director and ensure the board receives a summary of what was learned and what, if anything, should be done to improve his or her effectiveness. The Center provides this service using our Leader 360° assessment tool.

Focus on Relational Health & Meaningful Work

Relational health precedes board health. Board members and directors need to focus on emotional and relational management. We find that leaders and board members who do not have reasonable relational management skills will create pain and conflict for themselves and others. The new name for this is "emotional intelligence." The old name for it was "Getting along with others!" Regardless of your approach to governing, the *people* in the positions make the difference. The best governance structure with the wrong people will still not work. An imperfect governance structure with the right people can work. The right people with the right attitudes can cover a multitude of missteps!

In their book, *Governance as Leadership* (2005), Richard P. Chait, William P. Ryan, and Barbara E. Taylor pose an interesting question: "What would be the single gravest consequence to your organization if your board did not meet or conduct board business in any way for a two-year period?" Would it affect anything? Or are the responsibilities you have given your board unimportant and unfulfilling? It is vital that board members feel that their work is meaningful in order for them to desire to remain in their position.

Chait, Ryan, and Taylor go on to depict how by tasking our boards with unsatisfying work, we essentially treat them as substitute teachers, important but unfulfilling.

> "In effect, by constructing their job around the fiduciary work of oversight, nonprofit organizations have placed board members in a position akin to that of a substitute teacher. As an institution, the substitute teacher works effectively. It assures school administrators and parents that children who might run amok in the absence of a teacher remain under control. But the work of the substitute teacher is singularly unattractive. Adherence to minimum standards—not trying to teach, but merely trying to keep order—is as (or more) challenging than actually teaching. It is also far less rewarding. Board members suffer from this substitute's dilemma. Society has essentially asked trustees to keep order. As a result, board members become disengaged. The more disengaged they become, the less likely trustees are to ensure accountability—the very reason we created boards in the first place. By asking for a little, we get even less." (Richard P. Chait, William P. Ryan, and Barbara E. Taylor, *Governance as Leadership*, 2005)

Meaningful work will help to engage and retain qualified board members!

Understand the Fiduciary Duties of Board Members

Although we hope your organization is able to steer clear of legal and financial challenges, it is important for board members to understand their fiduciary duties (being responsible for something placed in their care or trust). The following is a summary of the four fiduciary duties of a nonprofit board noted in Richard Hammar's *Church Law & Tax Report* (November/December 2014).

Due Care

A director or an officer of a nonprofit "has a continuing fiduciary duty of loyalty and care in the management of the [corporation's] fiscal and investment affairs" (Hammar).

To avoid breaching the fiduciary duty of due care:

- Attend all meetings of the board
- Thoroughly review the agenda and financial statements before meetings
- Dissent from board actions which you have serious misgivings and insist your objection be recorded in the minutes
- Provide all members with a copy of the minutes soon after
- Ensure all actions are authorized and consistent with the organization's bylaws

Prudent Investing

Directors are only accountable to the court if "an investment decision was not based on the care an ordinarily prudent person in a like position would exercise under similar circumstances" (Hammar). To avoid violating the fiduciary duty of due care in investing, members should use an investment committee, create an investment policy, avoid risky investments, and avoid investing in companies that a board member has a personal interest in.

Loyalty

The fiduciary duty of loyalty "requires that any transaction between the board and one of its directors be fully disclosed, approved by the board without the vote of the interested director, and fair and reasonable to the corporation" (Hammar). A board member needs to offer his/her product or service at a fair and reasonable price to stay in the boundaries of this ruling; it doesn't have to be at the lowest price. Actions of the board member should not be secretive either.

Obedience

It is the duty of the board of directors "to ensure that the mission of the charitable corporation is carried out" through making sure the organization retains its tax exemption, is in compliance with its bylaws, and is in compliance with the federal, state, and local laws (Hammar).

Practice the 7 Vital Signs of Board/Staff Synergy

Healthy and effective leadership is pictured in the seven visual signs shown below. This tool can serve as a valuable assessment and discussion resource for your board and director.

COMPETENCY	Leaders at the staff and board level who manifest skill, integrity and maturity
VISION	Compelling, agreed upon direction and priorities
TRUST	An environment where leadership has earned trust and works to retain it
RELATIONSHIP	Leaders who care about one another and cover one another's backs
AUTHORITY	A board that hires the right people, grants authority, and retains limited control
CANDOR	Leaders who speak with transparency and encourage others to do the same
GRACE	Leaders who extend grace and forgiveness when disappointed

Know When to Seek Help

From our experience, it is better to seek professional guidance from a third party before problems arise. This assistance can be in the areas of board education and board development. It is especially critical to seek professional help early if conflict is emerging or if the board or director are not functioning effectively.

A healthy board is a critical factor in the effectiveness of the organization it governs. If the board is not attentive, there will be no accountability and mishaps could easily follow. If the board is belligerent, the staff of the organization will become worn out. Creating an effective board is not a simple task; it requires focus, perseverance and clear communication in all areas. A well-functioning board can pave the way for the organization to produce abundant results.

"

If you're not sure where you are going, you're liable to end up someplace else.

ROBERT F. MAGER

Section 2: Where Are We?

Assessing the Present & Planning for Action

Organizational Vision & Momentum

by Jay R. Desko, Ph.D.

Simple Is Best

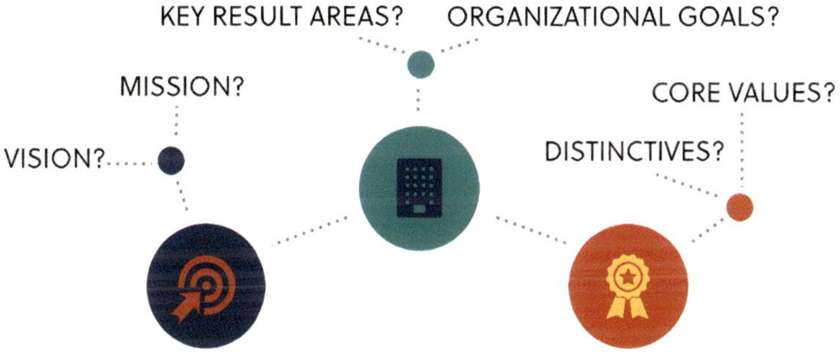

As consultants, we often work with clients who feel a bit confused and stuck. –Confused because what they read and hear is telling them they need some or all of the above pieces. This is often reflected in statements such as: "A seminar leader told me I need a vision statement and mission statement. Do I?" –And stuck because they aren't sure what is really needed and what is missing. This is often reflected in statements such as: "I just want an organization that has momentum. How can I get there?" For example, let's take a look at Jack. He, his leadership team, and his board had been working for over a year on vision and direction for their organization. They created a vision statement, a generic mission statement, a set of ten core values, and three organizational priorities. However, now they were more confused than ever about what this really meant to their organization, and their effort resulted in little action or momentum for the organization. But, they did have a nice looking, thick notebook that was impressive but irrelevant!

From our experience, organizations are spending far too much time working on organizational statements and lengthy documents and far too little time on truly defining a vision and priorities that result in both action and momentum. We find a clear correlation between the complexity and length of the vision and related elements with the likelihood that it is not leading to any meaningful action. The time consuming work, talk, and planning meetings can sometimes mask deeper issues of confusion, fear, political dynamics, and incompetence. But it can give the illusion that meaningful work is being done.

3 Elements Needed for a High Momentum Organization

There are many factors that play into organizational momentum including God's choosing to do something big or special in spite of the leaders or circumstances. However, that is more often the exception than the rule. From our consulting experience, there are three elements that are present in high momentum organizations.

When you have the convergence of credible leaders, compelling vision, and effective execution, a powerful and positive reaction takes place that results in attracting great talent, financial donations, and investing.

Credible Leaders

Credible leaders are those who are viewed as trustworthy and proven. These are leaders who employees, followers and donors believe can and will do the right things and do things right. While character is a vital part of this, there is much more. Credible leaders:

- Always act with integrity
- Do what they say they will do
- Admit mistakes quickly and do their best to correct them
- Solve problems and help others do the same
- Recognize (publicly and privately) others' contributions

- Listen to suggestions and feedback
- Share information openly and freely
- Are accessible and visible
- Have a track record of delivering results

Compelling Vision

Often referred to as a preferred future, a compelling vision is a short descriptive picture of what your organization is aiming for. Some books will tell you that you need to have a mission statement *and* a vision statement. Don't believe it. While there can be a difference between the two (mission describes your reason for existence while vision describes your future) and there is nothing wrong with having both of these statements, there are plenty of successful organizations that work off of one unifying description of why they exist and where they are going. Many organizations have both a mission and vision statement, but there is minimal difference between them in actual function or feel.

For example, look at the mission and vision statements of Make-A-Wish, an exceptional nonprofit that grants wishes to children who are facing life-threatening illnesses.

MAKE-A-WISH MISSION

We grant the wishes of children with life-threatening medical conditions to enrich the human experience with hope, strength and joy.

MAKE-A-WISH VISION

That people everywhere will share the power of a wish.

While there is a difference between the two statements, I am not convinced the difference is worth spending a hundred hours of planning, debate and discussion over just to create two different statements. Make-A-Wish has touched the lives of thousands of very sick children. Both statements are meaningful, yet it is hard to know if there would be any measurable loss by merging them into one.

Another example is the mission and vision of Jesus. How clearly can you differentiate between what the Bible describes as his mission and vision?

JESUS

"Jesus came to seek and save the lost." (Luke 19:10)

"I have come that they may have life, and have it to the full." (John 10:10)

"On hearing this, Jesus said to them, 'It is not the healthy who need a doctor, but the sick. I have not come to call the righteous, but sinners.'" (Mark 2:17)

If Jesus didn't get worked up about perfectly defined mission and vision statements, maybe we shouldn't either.

Children's Hospital of Philadelphia is the oldest and highest ranking children's hospital in the United States. It has accomplished this with one unifying and concise statement that it calls its mission:

CHILDREN'S HOSPITAL OF PHILADELPHIA

Children's Hospital of Philadelphia strives to be the world leader in the advancement of healthcare for children by integrating excellent patient care, innovative research and quality professional education into all of its programs.

I know some will have strong feelings about this, and that is OK. In my opinion, whether you choose to call it mission, vision, or both, it is most important that you simply answer these questions:

1. Where are we going?
2. What are we doing?
3. Why are we doing it?
4. How are we going to get there?
5. Are we there yet?
6. How can I help?

The answers to these questions should fit on one sheet of paper with a lot of white space! The answers often result in **a clear and compelling direction with 3-5 priorities.** We often call this "the playbook." If you get this far, your likelihood of experiencing progress will grow exponentially, regardless of how many cool and creative statements you have.

Leadership is not about statements; it's about purposeful action!

Effective Execution

One of the unfortunate and unnecessary ways a leader harms his credibility and the momentum of his organization is by not ensuring that a decision or plan, for which he is responsible, is carried out in a timely manner. In their book *Execution, The Discipline of Getting Things Done* (2002), Larry Bossidy and Ram Charan note that execution is the major job of a leader, and it must be a key element of the organization's culture. So, if execution is so important, why does it sometimes not happen? The following are the top reasons:

1. There is **no buy-in** by some of the key power-brokers in the organization.
2. The culture and key leaders accept **excuses** and fail to hold people **accountable.**
3. Sometimes, people **coast** and **evade** the hard work that needs to be done.
4. The required **resources** are not being provided.
5. No one is assigned **ownership** for implementation.
6. There is **fear** of failure and consequence.

No matter how compelling the vision, it is irrelevant if action is not taken. Helen Keller is believed to have once said, "A vision without action is only a dream!"

How Momentum Really Works

Whether you are a church, business or a nonprofit such as a school or social service agency, it is our belief that organizational momentum most often results from the convergence of these elements: the right people, compelling vision, and context and opportunity. It is important to remember that we, as fallen people, cannot fabricate momentum in our organization. At times, we are even confounded by the momentum that we see since, humanly-speaking, there would be no explanation for it.

One of the most important things we have learned about organizational momentum is just how fast it can change. Organizations were once much more resilient to large and rapid fluctuations of momentum than they are today. It is critically important for leaders to monitor the signs of positive and negative momentum markers which are depicted below.

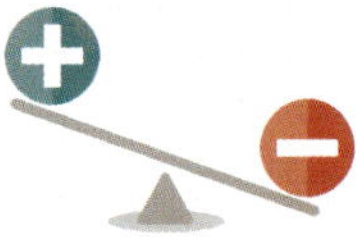

POSITIVE MOMENTUM	VS	NEGATIVE MOMENTUM
Can do no wrong	1	Can do no right
Infectious optimism	2	Growing cynicism
Increasing credibility	3	Decreasing credibility
Confidence & celebration	4	Fear & defeat
Sense of voice & ownership	5	Control & forced "positivism"
Positive numbers & outcomes	6	Negative numbers & outcomes

6 Ways to Kill Organizational Vision & Momentum

1. Too much talk, too little action

Leaders, staffs and boards sometimes have a tendency to talk, analyze and plan themselves to a slow, painful death. While conversation, analysis and planning is vital, it can sometimes become a detriment to producing momentum if it does not result in timely action.

"The best decision-makers are those who are willing to suffer the most over their decisions but still retain the ability to be decisive." –Psychiatrist M. Scott Peck

2. Too many voices

While collaboration and seeking input from others is beneficial in a visioning process, you can reach a point of oversaturation. Like a plant, water is vital for growth, but too much and it drowns. There is a difference between how many voices are needed in creating a vision and related strategy versus testing the vision by seeking input and buy-in.

3. Too complex a planning process

Complexity is often the death blow to many visioning processes. When the process involves 30 people working through six phases spread out over 12 months, you likely have too complex a process. Remember, unless you are planning for an extraordinarily large undertaking such as a once in a lifetime capital expansion, merger or acquisition, or building a four-star hotel on Mars, vision planning does not need to be as complex as it is often made out to be.

4. Too much confusion over roles

Whose job is it to cultivate the vision of the organization? Whoever has the gifts and passion worth following! While it is a senior leader or leadership team's job to *ensure* there is a compelling vision, that does not necessarily mean they are the *only ones* who possess those qualities. Quite often, the best vision is already resident in the DNA of the organization and its people. The leadership's primary job is to be listening and discerning what that vision is and how to feed it.

5. Too much fear of risk

In their book *Flight of the Buffalo* (2008), authors James Belasco and Ralph Stayer write, "Change is hard because people overestimate the value of what they have—and underestimate the value of what they may gain by giving that up."

We have seen this too often in churches and other organizations where the leaders fear losing the safety and stability of what already is and therefore, find dignified and legitimate sounding excuses to avoid any major risk or change. Leaders who are driven by anxiety create an anxious organization, one where political factions and conflict grow due to the indecisiveness of the leadership. In other words, the fear of conflict that leads to inaction will most likely result in the very conflict leaders are trying to avoid!

6. Too much confidence

In Jim Collins' excellent book, *How the Mighty Fall* (2009), he describes the stages that lead to the demise of organizations. The first stage in the process is pride that grows out of previous success. Success is wonderful to experience, but the more you have of it, the greater the risk of a leader or organization beginning to believe they cannot fail. Such confidence usually tips over into an arrogant spirit, one that feels invincible, one that does not seek counsel, and one that over-extends itself.

9 Ways to Build & Sustain Vision & Momentum

1. Protect the organization from you!

The fears, insecurities, ego needs and arrogance of one or more leaders can be the single greatest harm to a high momentum organization.

2. Build a great leadership environment and team.

A blend of catalysts, experts, and testers working in a high trust environment can do amazing things!

3. Face your organization's reality; don't avoid it.

Every organization has ups and downs. However, it cannot improve until it honestly faces its weaknesses and opportunities.

4. Swing for singles, enjoy home runs.

Many organizations strive for home runs. However, most momentum comes from the convergence of small opportunities, small actions, and small successes over a long period.

5. Compare your organization to your vision, not to others.

Comparison can be deadly to momentum. Other organizations are not your measure – your vision is.

6. Experiment when you are strong, not when you are weak.

The best time to try new ideas for momentum is when the organization is healthy, having both energy and resources. Even when an organization is weak, however, it must still experiment. Not experimenting will likely lead to further decline.

7. If everyone is talking about it, think twice about doing it.

Often, organizations adopt programs and events because so many others do. Sustainable momentum is seldom built this way.

8. Guard momentum since it is hard to acquire and easy to lose.

It only takes a few hurtful events or bad decisions to lose it.

9. Remember that success is often a greater enemy than being average.

When an organization is experiencing momentum, its leaders can become proud, resulting in arrogance and failure to continue learning.

As consultants, we have seen far too many organizations slow their own momentum down by getting stuck on the less important details. The most important steps you can take are to define your vision in a way that paints a clear and compelling picture of your future, while appointing leaders who are trustworthy and have a history of proven performance. Once you have those two factors in place, outlining the other aspects like values, goals and result areas will come much more easily.

Planning: The Art of Assessment

by David A. Marks, D.Min.

7 Reasons Why Plans Fail

Many leaders and executives have all but abandoned the idea of strategic planning, regarding it as nothing more than an exercise in futility. The amount of time and money spent on planning appears for most to be the proverbial rat-hole, sucking resources out of the organization and yielding little or no value. The thick binders that sit on the shelves of their offices are constant reminders of the colossal waste they once called "long-term planning." The ROI (Return on Investment) makes it difficult to justify the effort of building up everybody's hopes, selling a vision, and rolling it out onto the launchpad where it goes up like a rocket and comes down like a rock. People go into silence about the failure and simply move on until they're ready to sell another new vision with a plan that won't work once again. Does this sound familiar? It should; according to a research study published in 2015 in the *Harvard Business Review*, only 8% of leaders are good at both strategy and execution.

From our observations, we can identify at least seven reasons why plans fail:

1. Leading without listening
2. Starting with the future instead of the past
3. Asking the wrong questions
4. Complexity rather than simplicity
5. Objectives without champions
6. Destinations without demarcation (metrics)
7. The illusion of pain-free planning

1. Leading Without Listening

Historically, planning was done as a top-down exercise. The people who controlled the resources were also assumed to be the ones who had the most knowledge, and as a result, they believed they possessed a superior ability to plan the future of the organization. So dominate was this way of thinking that most viewed it as the responsibility of leaders and not just the privilege and power of leaders. Fortunately, we now have many examples of excellent leaders who have taken a different approach to planning. They understand the value of the bubble-up process where voices from within and from without the organization are sought early in the process.

TOP DOWN VOICE VS. BOTTOM UP VOICE

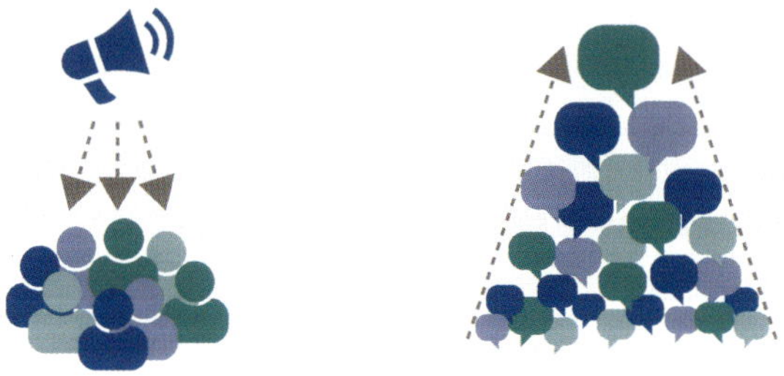

These leaders believe that by listening at the base level of where the organization actually has to function, they can learn valuable lessons that will ultimately inform their leadership and increase the odds of developing plans that can actually be implemented.

Fear of critique may be one of the hidden motivators behind leaders who want to cast a fresh vision without input from those who are lower on the organizational chart. They do not want anybody throwing cold water on their brilliant ideas or raising objections based on the current state of the organization. The concept is easy if the leader's ego does not prevent it. Say it out loud a few times in the correct order: **LISTEN · LEARN · LEAD; LISTEN · LEARN · LEAD; LISTEN · LEARN · LEAD.** I suspect that leaders who try to lead without listening still have a thing or two to learn.

2. Starting with the Future Instead of the Past

Effective planning could stand to learn a great deal from the Hollywood blockbuster *Back to the Future*. To truly affect your future by design, planning a trip to the past is necessary. When assessing organizations, our consultants at The Center want to learn everything we can about how the current state of affairs has been shaped by the decisions and events of the past. Just like people, organizations have a DNA. To ignore that fact is to do so to your own harm. Planning that does not take time to capture the leading lessons from the past, good and bad, will likely generate a plan that is both inadequate and impotent since accurately assessing where you are currently is the required first step to navigating where you want to go in the future.

Like a GPS (Global Positioning System), good planning only works when it can identify your current location.

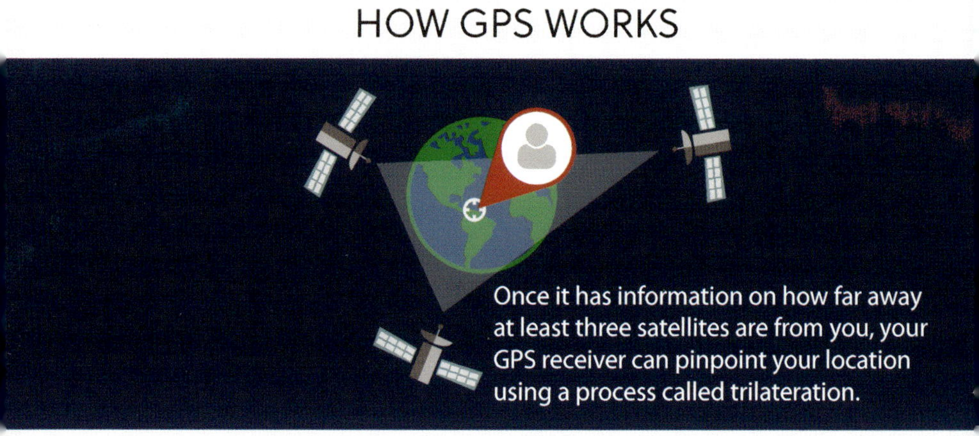

To stretch that analogy a bit further, GPS satellites are used to get an objective and unhindered view of the actual coordinates. Similarly, the consultants at The Center are frequently used for the same purpose, to facilitate good planning from a perspective that cannot be fully attained by those in the "driver seat" of the organization.

The late Stephen Covey famously instructed his readers to "start with the end in mind" (*The 7 Habits of Highly Effective People*, 2013). What would-be-planners often forget is he first instructed them to take a good, hard look at themselves and figure out what made them tick before trying to plan a different future for themselves.

Consider the following questions to help you assess how the past and present may influence the future plans for your organization.

PAST:

Know your DNA. Explore these questions regarding the history of your organization.

1. Do we possess an accurate written history? The longer an organization has been in existence, the more important it is that someone captures an accurate record of successes, failures, significant people, key decisions, motives, and the mission and vision of the founders.
2. What made our past strategies unique from our contemporaries?
3. Is the past currently viewed with disdain or delight?
4. What are considered the "glory days" or the best days in our history? Why?
5. What are the scars or "dark days" of the past that created regret or marked missed opportunities?
6. What from the past still significantly affects the organization today? (Positively or negatively)

PRESENT:

Solicit a broad base of voices from inside and outside of the organization to populate the four quadrants on the following chart. Agility in planning is essential because it allows planners to appropriately adjust for factors that will most certainly impact the organization positively and negatively. Just like carrying an umbrella when the weather forecast predicts heavy rains, so should organizations plan for disruptive technologies or for an aging workforce, for example. The value of this type of modified SWOT analysis is that it allows planners to: **accentuate**/maximize their strongest attributes; prepare to **adopt** more quickly to coming advancements; **adapt** or find alternatives to navigate obstacles that may work against the success of the organization; and **address** boldly the areas within the organization where improvement is needed in order to maximize effectiveness or optimize new opportunities.

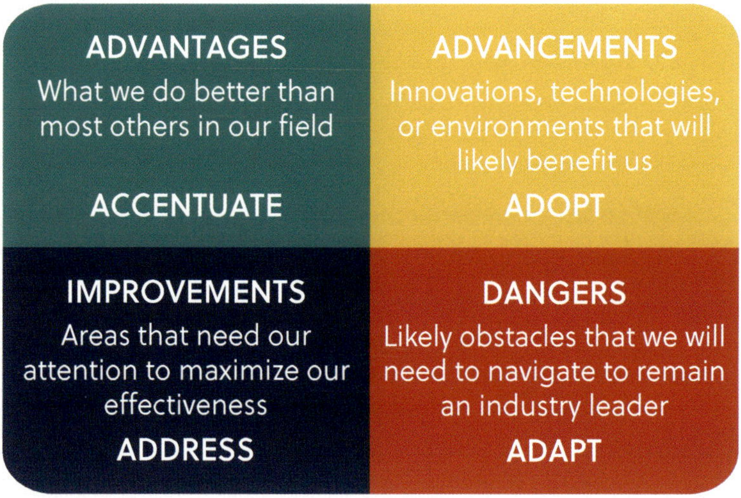

3. Asking the Wrong Questions

The only thing worse than not asking any questions while planning is to ask the *wrong* questions. There is certainly an art to asking the right questions at the right time of the right people. To find the *critical thinkers* in the group, simply listen to their questions. Their questions bring clarity to the planning process. But then there are *critical stinkers*. This group of unwelcomed participants often serve to do nothing more than obstruct and elongate the process. It would seem as if this group has an endless stream of irrelevant questions that reveal their personal preferences and desire to control the conversation. Innovative ideas have little hope of implementation.

There are six questions that will help planners to assess the worthiness of their plan. The six questions become the litmus test as to whether or not the plan is sustainable. John Kotter, a leading authority and best-selling author on leading change in organizations, suggests a benchmark of having 70% of any given constituency that is able to tell you what the vision of the organization is all about. For instance, you have a well-structured plan if seven out of every ten people in your organization can answer the BIG SIX questions in 20 seconds. Yes, you read that correctly... answer six questions in 20 seconds.

1. Where are we going?
2. What are we doing?
3. Why are we doing it?
4. How are we going to get there?
5. Are we there yet?
6. How can I help?

We have noticed that organizations that strive for this benchmark have plans that call for commitment and are concise, clear, well communicated, and compelling.

4. Complexity Rather than Simplicity

COMPLEX VS. SIMPLE

You may shake your head in disbelief at the notion that a great action plan can and should be captured on a single piece of paper! This is true for multi-million dollar corporations as well as individuals planning their own future. Remember, most strategic plans never get implemented. We suspect this is due to plans being too complex and having too many contingencies. It is far better to discern the top 2 to 3 priorities and create a plan to accomplish those in 24 to 36 months than to have an all-encompassing plan with so many moving pieces that very few can comprehend it. Using the principle of the Law of Diminishing Returns, less is more when it comes to actually implementing a plan. The odds of acting on any more than three or four main priorities during any three-year period is likely to jeopardize all of the priorities. The following chart makes this point.

LAW OF DIMINISHING RETURNS

Number of Goals Attempted	2-3	4-10	11-20
	↓	↓	↓
Number of Goals Achieved	2-3	1-2	0

5. Objectives without Champions

A concert of critical factors needs to blend seamlessly to move organizations forward. One of those vital factors is leadership. John Maxwell accurately stated, "Everything rises and falls on leadership." A compelling vision without a credible leader is likely to remain a dream rather than a reality. It sounds quite easy, but actually finding people with passion and expertise for a particular priority may prove to be difficult. It is far better to delay initiating a priority than to launch a priority without a champion. Managers are important guardians of protocols and processes, but priority leaders provide motivation, innovation, and often have broader authority within the whole system and are able to assure that funding, space, and time remain available. For this reason, many organizations enter a season of leadership development prior to doing extensive action planning.

6. Destinations without Demarcation (Metrics)

On a road trip, you frequently calculate how many miles until you arrive, and at a sporting event, you carefully monitor the score. In planning, it is equally important to know your mile markers or your scorecard. Any plan that does not have incremental measuring points has already paved the pathway to defeat. Peter Drucker is often quoted as saying, "You can't manage what you can't measure." Drucker means that you can't know whether or not you are successful unless success is defined and tracked. Strangely, organizations have a propensity to do what I call pie-in-the-sky planning. This planning is characterized by great optimism and energy but does not have credibility because it lacks accountability for any KPIs (key performance indicators). Charismatic leaders can often convince people that a goal is attainable when in reality success has not even been clearly defined (Example A). Metrics that can be monitored help guide an organization to the “bulls-eye” (Example B).

7. The Illusion of Pain-Free Planning

Saying YES means saying NO. One of the most pronounced benefits of developing a priority-based action plan is the freedom it gives to leaders to accept and reject the constant stream of new ideas and opportunities that present themselves. I like to visualize a well-crafted plan as having Velcro on one side and Teflon on the other. The things that benefit and fuel the plan are like Velcro and the plan allows them to stick. Ideas that are tangential to the plan can be easily dismissed; they slide off like a fried egg in a Teflon pan.

Obviously there needs to be exceptions, especially when a new resource or new opportunity presents itself, but those should be rarities, not the norms. The discipline to stay focused on the plan that has already taken into account the bandwidth of the calendar, checkbook, and the workforce should not be easily dismissed. To do so often puts the whole plan in jeopardy.

Accurately assessing the pillars and the pitfalls in the planning process is essential. The exercise at the end of this chapter will provide you with an excellent tool, but it is not pain-free. The goal in any pre-planning assessment process is to identify what I like to call cousins and casualties.

Cousins are those elements within the organization that can be easily retooled to support and promote the new priorities. In other words, they fit well with the preferred future outlined in the plan.

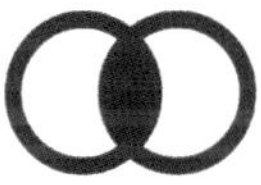

COUSINS

Casualties, on the other hand, are those areas that have served their purpose but are no longer adding high value to the organization or they no longer fit with the preferred future of the organization as outlined in its plan.

CASUALTIES

They are like lead boots are to a swimmer – they use up the organization's resources on programs, procedures, or people that no longer contribute to the success of the organization's mission. In his book *Necessary Endings* (2011), Dr. Henry Cloud notes that while hard, endings are an important part of renewal. From our observations over the years, we have assisted organizations facing such a season; they sometimes make the mistake of continually searching for a "perfect" and "peaceful" ending. This is nice but seldom possible. Too much introspection and reflection seldom produces renewed health and can have the unintended consequences of too much focus on "me" and "us." Peter Drucker gives this powerful analogy:

> "To get at the new and better, you have to throw out the old, outworn, obsolete, no longer productive, as well as the mistakes, failures, and misdirections of efforts of the past. 'As long as the patient eliminates there is a chance. But once the bowels and bladder stop, death does not take long.' If organizations cannot get rid of their waste products, they poison themselves. They must organize abandonment, a most difficult thing to do, because most organizations develop a strong emotional attachment to the products they make." (Peter Drucker, *Managing for the Future*, 2013)

Gap Analysis Exercise

This tool can help you recognize and "plug" holes that are draining energy from your top organizational priorities. The premise is based on the thought that the greatest efforts and the highest priority of resources should be given to the areas that are most essential to the overall health and effectiveness of the organization. There is a level of subjectivity that is required, so it is wise to have several people participate in the exercise. Using the Program Alignment Gap Analysis chart on page 89, follow these steps.

Step 1: List all the activities and programs of your organization. (Anything that takes time, money, facilities, or paid staff to accomplish.)

Step 2: Assign a priority level to every program.

- **Level 1 Priority – ESSENTIAL:** Limit the assignment of Level 1 activities or programs to those that are absolutely integral to your mission, vision, core values, and unique DNA. Caution: The discussion about level assignments can be polarizing to a group. People generally believe what they are doing is most important.
- **Level 2 Priority – IMPORTANT:** These are activities and programs that are viewed as important for health, growth and momentum, but are NOT absolute essentials. They are important because they are catalytic in nature. These may be tied to your current priorities and goals.
- **Level 3 Priority – ENJOYED:** Every organization has activities or programs that are non-essential or not truly important to the overall health, growth, and momentum of the organization but are still valued and enjoyed by the membership.
- **Level 4 Priority – TOLERATED:** Often labeled as "sacred cows," these types of programs have served their usefulness to the organization and are now viewed by most as a hindrance rather than a help. For political or economic reasons, these activities remain.

Step 3: Assign a resource draw factor to each of the programs. For those program areas that require a high amount of resources (human, financial, time, etc.), put an **H** for high draw. Use **M** for medium draw, and **L** for low resource drawing programs.

Step 4: Assign an effectiveness grade to each of the identified program areas. Efficiency in this step means assessing the effectiveness (overall impact) of each area according to what it is designed to be accomplishing for the organization considering the amount of resources it requires to function optimally. To asses, use the following letter grades:

A. This area is functioning at its highest potential. Little or no improvement is needed.
B. This program is a solid performer. It adds good value to the organization. There is room for improvement over time.
C. This program is average at best. There is plenty of room for improvement and the sooner the better.
D. Without improvement, this area will hurt the momentum of other programs. Improvement is needed immediately, or this area should be eliminated or completely overhauled.
F. This program should be eliminated. It no longer serves the purpose for which it was created and absorbs resources and passion from other programs.

Step 5: Identify an Alignment Action for each and every program listed. Decide upon one of three actions: will you **(I) improve it, (C) cut it, or (M) maintain it** to make sure that your resources are correctly focused on what is most important? For example, those areas that are a Level 1 or Level 2 and have a high to medium resource draw, but are not getting efficiency grades of a B+ or better, should be improved. Cut the resource draining activities that are Level 3 or Level 4, and then reallocate and focus the resources to your Level 1 and Level 2 programs. Doing very well in Levels 3 and 4 at the expense of effectiveness in Levels 1 and 2 is a deterrent to the success of your organization.

PROGRAM ALIGNMENT GAP ANALYSIS

List All Programs	Priority Level (1,2,3,4)	Resource Draw (H,M,L)	Effectiveness Grade (A,B,C,D,F)	Alignment Action (I,C,M)

Conduct an Autopsy

Conduct an autopsy on past strategic planning done by your organization using the seven indicators of foolish planning:

1. Leading without listening
2. Starting with the future instead of the past

3. Asking the wrong questions
4. Complexity rather than simplicity
5. Objectives without champions
6. Destinations without demarcation (metrics)
7. The illusion of pain-free planning

Wordsmithing Exercise

Before you begin the actual planning process, it will serve you well to begin practicing writing priority statements. Identify two or three likely priorities for your organization, and put them in the "best" format as illustrated below.

Good:
The United States is entering the space race. (1955)

Better:
The United States will be the world leader in space exploration. (1957)

Best:
"I believe that this nation should commit itself to achieving the goal, before this decade is out, of landing a man on the Moon and returning him safely to the Earth." –President John F. Kennedy (1961)

Formula:
We are going from **A** to **B** by **C**.

Creating a Healthy Planning Environment

by David A. Marks, D.Min.

The Planning Environment

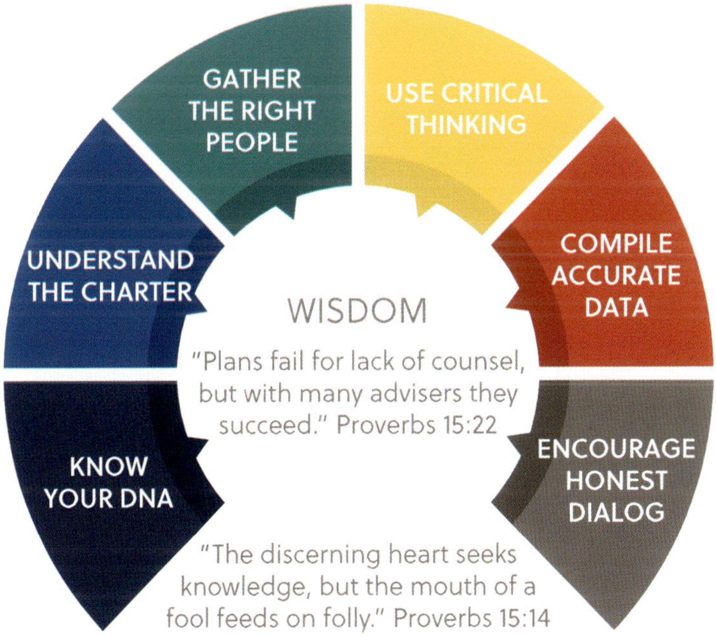

Calendar planning has become routine, budget planning has become routine, and setting staff goals for the coming year has become routine. THEREFORE, action planning has become irrelevant, unwelcomed, and unnecessary since it is intended to *precede* all of those routine disciplines. Action planning is meant to be a leader, not a follower. Once you have cemented your budget, calendar, and goals, you have rendered action planning impotent unless all of those elements are informed and empowered by the action planning process!

Action planning, by its very definition, should be a dynamic and fluid process. To illustrate, imagine an airplane pilot sitting in the cockpit of an airplane that is full of fuel, passengers, and loaded with luggage and cargo but doesn't know the flight plan. Where are we going? When is it our turn to take off? Do I have a crew that knows what they're doing once we're wheels up? Why do some passengers think we are going to Fort Lauderdale, Florida and others think we are going to Fargo, North Dakota? Perhaps that scene seems too bizarre, but the reality is many organizations are simply maintaining routines rather than planning the order of operations that will move their mission forward from Point A to Point B. Chaos exists where an action plan does not.

The most basic action planning can focus an organization and move it from chaos to a coordinated effort that brings satisfaction to those involved, and in many cases brings profitability/fruitfulness to the organization as it achieves its mission's objectives. A valid action plan brings clarity to these seven questions.

1. **What** changes will be occurring?
2. **Why** is this helpful?

3. **Who** will carry it out?
4. **When** will it take place, and for how long?
5. **Where** is this happening?
6. **What** resources (i.e., money, space, staff) are needed to carry out the changes?
7. **Who** should know what and when? (communication roll-out)

Results are often predicated on environment. Good fishing takes place on the water, not the desert sands; the best surgeries are performed in operating rooms, not playgrounds; and outstanding action planning happens as a product of wisdom, not by gathering a variety of unrelated opinions. The following six factors are present when wisdom prevails in the action planning process.

Know Your DNA

Good planning does not begin with an empty sheet of paper hoping a brilliant new idea for the future strikes like lightning out of heaven. The best fertilizer for the future is found in analyzing what has happened in the past and what is currently happening in the present context. Ignore your DNA to your own harm. Like all living things, organizations also have DNA which directly shapes the type of culture that the organization develops in its particular context. Its structures, governance, practices, and principles all emanate from its internal coding, i.e. the things that have shaped the nature, values, history, and, to some extent, the organization's future. Over time, various events, people, and the problems solved alter the way the DNA is expressed and the organization's direction. To illustrate, a newborn baby acts very different than when that same child becomes a teenager. The DNA is the same, but the experience is very different.

The Center consultants have designed an instrument to help leaders and planners better understand how proposed changes will be effected by the internal compass of an organization. Built on Cameron and Quinn's Organizational Cultural Assessment Instrument (OCAI), participants evaluate ten specific areas where competing values are viewed from the lens of the past, present, and future. Planners often underestimate the effects changes will have, especially if the changes mark a new philosophical direction that is in contrast to past values. Too much change too quickly will likely be met with more resistance than incremental changes that are consistent with the organization's DNA.

Questions to ask about culture:

- Why was this organization started?
- What is the leadership structure?
- What is the governance model?
- Who needs to approve changes?
- What is the funding model?
- What types of changes will be intolerable?

CHARTING YOUR ORGANIZATION'S DNA

Your answers to questions in the following ten categories will determine where your organization falls on the chart below.

Leader Style	**Effectiveness Criteria**
Methods	**Follower Attitude**
Leader Values	**Workplace "Feel"**
Primary Focus	**Biggest Fear**
Leadership Environment	**Follower Behavior**

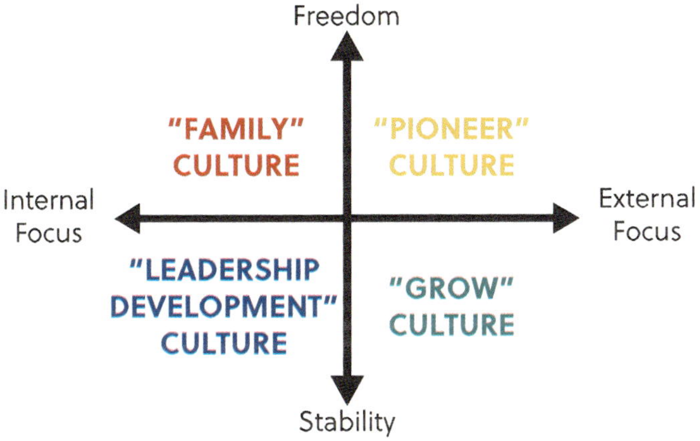

Understand the Charter

Every army needs to know its marching orders; this is especially true for a planning team. A team charter quickly focuses the team around its deliverables, aligns expectations, and eliminates the needless confusion that often manifests itself with subtle passive aggressive posturing or outright conflict, thus derailing the planning process. The authorizing agency may be the CEO, department head, the board, or other entities that have the positional right to assemble a planning team. If a charter is not provided, the team should use their first meeting or two to create one and submit it for approval to be sure expectations are the same and everyone involved is on the same page.

A well-written team charter should include the following:

- The main objective (final deliverable) of this team is...
- The team has been authorized by and reports directly to...
- The team is composed of the following people and these roles...
- It is expected that full team members will invest approximately ____ hours per ____ and the estimated time for the planning phase is ____ (this may be expressed in terms of frequency and length of scheduled meetings).
- The team has the authority to... (the scope of your work is_____ but not______)
- The following boundaries are in place... (helps define how much risk is acceptable)
- The team has access to the following resources and support...
- The work of the team is to be presented by (date) to _____ in the format of _____ (oral, written, etc).
- The team's work is complete, and the group is to be dissolved when... (brings clarity if it ends with planning or continues into communication of implementation phases)

PLANNING TEAM CHARTER EXAMPLE

The Priority Identification Team (PIT Crew) has been formed to identify the top three priorities for Acme Technology Company. The team is to be comprised of each of the department heads and one designate of their choice from their department. Jonathan Meyers from HR will be the team leader assisted by Sandy Smith from Finance. The team is schedule to meet each Monday for the next three months from 8:30 AM to 12:00 noon.

A written report from the entire team outlining the rationale for the identified priorities is to be presented to the Executive Team no later than May 1, 20--. Please include any data that is used to support the recommendations. It is NOT necessary for you to provide specific strategies and tactics with your report unless they naturally occur as a component of your research. A different team will be appointed for that task. Your current team will be disbanded following the approval of the report by the Executive Team.

Thank you for your service.

Gather the Right People

The composition of the planning team will prove to be significant to the success of the project. Each member of the group should know and be able to articulate why they are on the team. Not all members are created equally, even if they have equal voice in the process. Some may possess great knowledge, a long institutional memory, superior technical skills, access to resources and/or data, high credibility among stakeholders, or hold positions in the organization that make it vital that they be included. If I know why you are on the team and you know why I am on the team, we have increased the mutual respect factor, we understand we have a zone in which we are considered the "best" on the team for that purpose(s), and we will likely feel more confident in our contributions to the team. Individuals also have natural bents, personality, and temperament factors to be considered. Additionally, a mix of the following attributes should be considered when populating the planning team:

- **Catalysts** – Known for action and multiplying leaders, raising the organization's capacity for growth.

- **Pros** – Known for possessing specialized knowledge relevant to the organization.

- **Dreamers** – Known for being future oriented, thinking big picture. Stretch an organization beyond its present state.

- **Connectors** – Known for encouragement, humor, and enthusiasm. Add joy to the meetings.

- **Testers** – Known for candor, assertiveness, and testing assumptions through questioning. Help guard against major mistakes.

- **Technicians** – Known for figuring out the "how" for the "what."

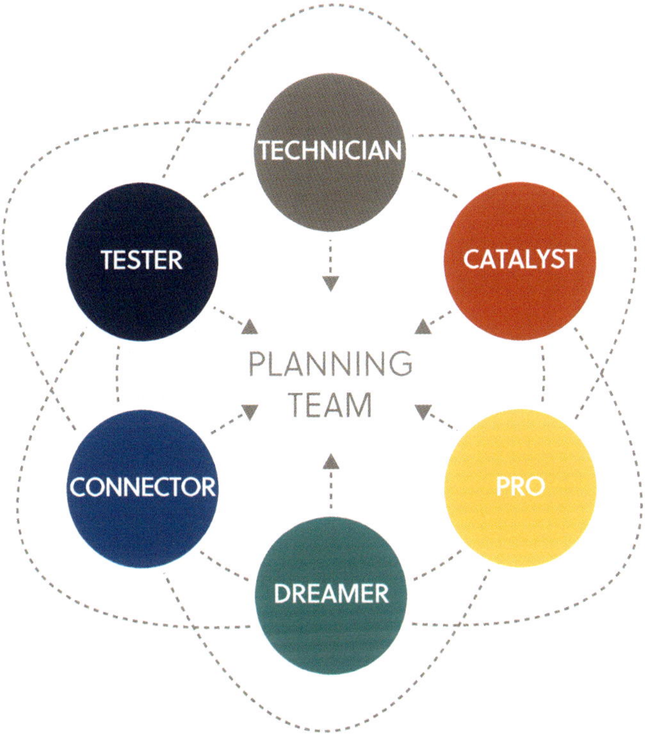

Of course, many planning teams use ad hoc members to add additional expertise from time to time without requiring them to be full team members. Teams are often able to assess quickly who is missing and then can seek their input. This was illustrated powerfully and comically when The Center was facilitating a planning session for a nonprofit organization with a strong desire to help young families with children, yet the youngest person on the planning team was sixty-years-old. Needless to say, they had no one who was able to advocate for what young families want or need. In subsequent meetings, they invited special guests from that demographic to inform their discussions. Good move!

Team formation is not an exact science, therefore, periodically reassess team membership. Keep in mind, teams need time to acclimate to each other and work through their unique differences. Bruce Tuckman, an early writer on team theory, outlined the often quoted stages of team development as "forming–storming–norming–performing." He and many others believe these phases are all necessary and inevitable in order for the team to grow, face up to challenges, tackle problems, find solutions, plan work, and deliver results. I suspect the length and the level of difficulty of the planning process will determine if all of these stages will manifest themselves. Nonetheless, we should be aware that they exist and may need to be patient to let a team evolve normally.

The expected value-added to the individual is often overlooked when assembling a team. This is especially true when using volunteers. Ideally, team members should feel honored to serve and appreciated for their contribution to the process.

Critical Thinking

Converting information into action is like using gasoline to make horsepower. It happens every day, all around the world, and it literally drives commerce. Yet, sparingly few people on the planet can explain the internal combustion engine and how it is that we can simply pump fuel into the back of the car and get wheels turning in the front of the car. So common and so refined is this process that we seldom think about it. Safe to say, a lot of critical thinking goes into the planning, engineering, and manufacturing of an ordinary automobile. Behind every highly effective organization, you can be assured there is a group of people doing the diligence of critical thinking. Everybody doesn't need to do it to enjoy the benefits of it, but when it is absent or dysfunctional, the end-users will eventually pay the price.

At the heart of critical thinking is an attempt at objective, unbiased analysis or evaluation of all the available information. Such thinking should not be limited to hard data alone as some have suggested. The desire is to follow the evidence wherever it may lead. This demeanor generally promotes a systematic approach to problem solving, inquisitiveness, even-handedness, and confidence in reasoning. In the planning process, it involves exploring many facets of the organization's culture and then offering a critique (a judgment or conclusion). Critical thinkers often help the planning team discern the real problem(s) to be solved and then pressure test (test assumptions) the proposed solutions against the identified problems. Not insignificantly, critical thinkers also help the group reflect on the possible unintended consequences resulting from the recommendations. I have observed that the best critical thinkers make fewer statements and ask more questions, not to be confused with the annoying individual who asks endless questions but provides no valid solution or opinion. Those strongly disposed toward critical thinking often serve the team by:

- Knowing what information or data to acquire
- Using inductive and deductive inquiry to isolate problems within problems

- Interpreting (making sense of) contradictory information
- Recognizing unstated assumptions and values behind generalizations
- Separating theory from fact and emotion from realities
- Sorting and scoring the priority or value of different kinds of information
- Reaching clear and credible conclusions

Examples of critical thinking questions are as follows (adapted from www.criticalthinking.org):

- For clarity: Can you give me an example?
- For accuracy: How can we verify or test that?
- For precision: Could you give me more details?
- For relevance: How does this relate to the problem?
- For depth: What are some of the difficulties we need to deal with?
- For breadth: Do we need to consider another point of view?
- For logic: Does all of this make sense together?
- For significance: Is this the most important problem to consider?
- For fairness: Do I have any vested interest in this issue?

Accurate Data

In the world of computer programing, there is an adage: "Garbage in, garbage out." Many plans have gone awry as a result of skewed data. The golden rule of carpentry is, "Measure twice, cut once." Why? Because carpenters know if you are off 1/8 of an inch now, you'll be off a foot later! Anecdotal input has a place but it cannot be the only type of input. Both qualitative and quantitative information will be needed.

Entering a season of active listening prior to planning is important on two fronts: it provides the data the team will need to do its work, and it begins to set the stage for solid buy-in during the implementation phase of the plan because such data reflects the realities of what your constituency is telling you. Our consultants like to use a triad of tools to listen to what the organization is actually saying about itself. Triangulating the data from the following three areas provides a comprehensive overview.

Document Review

Some organizations are more transparent than others in sharing their data. Gather as much as you can prior to the first meeting of the team. Data introduced to "prove a point" during the planning process can be incomplete. The following types of documentation will give the planning team insight into the DNA of the organization.

- Historical documents that outline the origins and chronology of the organization
- Financials, i.e. "follow the money"
- Minutes or records of key decisions, conflicts, capital campaigns, etc.
- Annual Reports (last five years is best)
- Results of past surveys
- Past mission and vision statements
- Current messaging on the website, social media, printed marketing, or communications to the public

Survey

In the case of sample size, more is generally better for planning purposes. The goal is to create a collective voice of the organization. A well-designed convenience sample survey can provide the equivalent of a fingerprint to help the planning team understand the uniqueness of the group. In addition to the inherent value of the data, it can also help the team avoid two classic mistakes: assuming a plan that worked in another context will work well in this one and over-weighting the opinion of individuals who believe they have the pulse on the larger group.

A word of caution: It is best to have a professional design and tabulate the survey data. There is an art and a science to survey design, and it can vary greatly from one type of organization to another. Many well-intentioned people have attempted to collect data, but in doing so, they inadvertently open Pandora's Box and release a swarm of defensive routines from their constituency which makes the desired future changes much more complicated. For instance, just because someone has a background in analytics does not make them an expert in organizational behavior. Collecting data is easy, making sense of it is not. Interpreting the data incorrectly will lead to regret!

Confidential Interviews

Every organization has high influence individuals. For one reason or another, they have the ear of many others. The qualitative data gained from their insights will prove to be valuable. As odd as it may appear, researchers have demonstrated that, when guaranteed strict confidentiality, most people will open up to a professional interviewer who is detached from the organization with a greater degree of transparency than to those who are a part of it. There is very little relational risk if the participant tells the stranger (the interviewer) the "real truth" about what they see and how they are feeling.

In addition to high influencers, consider interviewing a cross-section of participants. Stakeholders, officers, staff, board members, consumers, vendors, and end-users can all add important perceptions.

A skilled consultant can properly assimilate the most important data from these listening methods into a profile the planning team can rely upon.

Honest Dialog

The starting point of honest conversation is mutual respect among the team members. Human dynamics are naturally complex and some personalities are more demonstrative than others. A good facilitator will help moderate the tone of the meetings and bring into check anyone that threatens the honest exchange of ideas or uses punishing behaviors against those who ask hard but important questions of the group. Disagreement is an important part of honest dialog. When there is an "elephant in the room" that is off limits to relevant discussion, the planning process is doomed. Assuring confidentiality to all who participate is an important covenant to be confirmed in the first meeting of the team.

Removing any one of the six factors of a healthy planning environment will most certainly compromise the product. Do yourself a favor and do a check-up using the chart on the next page. Effective action planning happens when all six factors are present!

A goal without a plan is just a dream... go make it happen!

NOTE: The planning process is very complex and works better with professional guidance from a neutral facilitator. Don't hesitate to contact The Center to learn more about how we can assist you through this process!

PLANNING ENVIRONMENT CHECK-UP

Key Factors	Excellent: Let's Go	Uncertain: Dig Deeper	Poor: Hold On
Know Your DNA			
Understand the Charter			
Gather the Right People			
Critical Thinking			
Accurate Data			
Honest Dialog			

"

The most difficult thing is
the decision to act...

AMELIA EARHART

Section 3:
What Do We Want to Accomplish?

Discerning & Deciding

Decision-Making Mistakes

by Jay Desko, Ph.D.

Avoid the Decision Traps

The following ten points outline traps that can easily undermine your decisions if you fall into them.

1. Holding too high of an opinion of you.

In his research on *Why Smart People Do Dumb Things* (1995), Dr. Mortimer Feinberg identified the "pillars of stupidity." The top three are pride, arrogance and narcissism. The writer of Proverbs affirms the same by telling us that pride leads to destruction (Proverbs 16:18). In *Harvard Business Review's 2006* article "The Hidden Traps in Decision Making," John S. Hammond, Ralph L. Keeney, and Howard Raiffa note, "Even though most of us are not very good at making estimates or forecasts, we actually tend to be overconfident about our accuracy. That can lead to errors in judgment and, in turn, bad decisions." Sometimes we as individuals can view ourselves as greater than we are. But sometimes, groups such as a board or team of staff can collectively do the same. Either way, the results are the same: acting over-confidently, failing to seek advice, assuming you are smarter than you really are, and ultimately, a whole lot of damage!

2. Failing to seek or listen to wise counsel.

"For lack of guidance a nation falls, but victory is won through many advisers." –Proverbs 11:14

It really is amazing how often even intelligent people can make important decisions without seeking any input. If someone was facing cancer or heart disease, would he try to resolve it himself? Perhaps if he was a fool. But most people would get at least one expert, if not two, to weigh in on what to do next. Yet, leaders often make important decisions, decisions that can have a significant impact on themselves and those whom they serve, and do so with little or no counsel. The technical term for this person is "fool"! However, when seeking wise counsel, be careful not to fall into what Hammond, Keeney, and Raiffa refer to as the confirming-evidence bias. "This bias leads us to seek out information that supports our existing instinct or point of view while avoiding information that contradicts it"("The Hidden Traps in Decision Making," *Harvard Business Review*, 2006).

3. Making decisions impulsively.

Some people really do struggle with impulse control. It may be related to food, spending, careers, dating, or speech. The common theme in lack of impulse control is choosing to do something without thinking about the consequences, both in the short and long term. This is often referred to as the "ready, fire, aim" approach. In business, entrepreneurs sometimes suffer from this, which is why they may go from rags to riches and back to rags, all in a matter of a few years! Self-control is noted over ten times in the Bible reminding us of its importance and of the dangers when it is lacking in our lives. Hammond, Keeney, and Raiffa give another reason to avoid making decisions impulsively: "When considering a decision, the mind gives disproportionate weight to the first information it receives. Initial impressions, estimates, or data anchor subsequent thoughts and judgements" ("The Hidden Traps in Decision Making," *Harvard Business Review* 2006).

4. Allowing the search for a "perfect" decision to create paralysis.

Some people struggle with making decisions impulsively, but there are others who struggle with the opposite. They constantly think: "Let's study this some more." The fear of a mistake can incapacitate us. It is admirable to desire to make a good decision, but it is often a lack of courage and lack of faith in God when we seek a *perfect* one. Paralysis can also be a result of avoiding making a hard decision due to fear of conflict. This is often the case when it comes to needing to fire an employee or confront poor performance. While there are times when waiting longer and praying more are appropriate, this can also be a sign of a leader, board, or team living in fear and avoiding any risks.

> "On an important decision, one rarely has 100% of the information needed for a good decision no matter how much one spends or how long one waits. And, if one waits too long, he has a different problem and has to start all over. This is the terrible dilemma of the hesitant decision maker." –Robert K. Greenleaf, *The Servant as Leader*, 2008

5. Facing a decision that exceeds the skills or mental/emotional capacity of the leadership.

Picture a 12-year-old junior high school student trying to decide what college to attend. Or, how about a 35-year-old carpenter trying to build a high tech manufacturing complex. Or a 91-year-old grandmother trying to select a new smart phone from 12 options in front of her! What do they all have in common? They are each facing a decision that may exceed their mental or emotional capacity. Leaders often will experience such decisions. Do I buy or sell? Do I hire or fire? Do I take on debt or not? Do I transition to another position or stay here? Do I restructure the staff or leave it as is? These are just a few examples, and quite often, leaders are faced with a number of such decisions all at once. As for Trap #2: Failing to seek or listen to wise counsel, leaders need to surround themselves with others who have experience and can help shed clarity on the situation.

6. Viewing questions as an enemy rather than a friend.

Over my years of consulting, I have heard many employees say that they are not willing to ask any questions of a supervisor because it is too risky. Even though the leader says she wants input and questions, the perception of those around her is that they will be punished if they do. Sometimes this is just an excuse team members use due to their own lack of courage or insecurity. However, we have seen on many occasions how a leader can become aggressive or defensive which sends the message: “Don’t question me!” Yet, without being questioned, a leader is much more likely to make poor decisions since he or she may not have thought through it or missed important information that could have improved the decision or prevented a damaging decision from being made.

7. Failing to understand and manage human dynamics.

I remember working with a board made up of incredibly intelligent people. I was trying to help them navigate a major decision, and in the midst of the meeting, they brought up a failed decision from a few years before. As I listened, I was fascinated by what took place. As they described it, the board had made a unanimous decision, but in reviewing it a few years later, the great majority of them did not actually like what they had decided at the time they decided it!

How does this happen? When you put two or more people together, the dynamics between the people can influence how a decision is made. According to Dr. Daniel Goleman, one of the leading researchers in emotional intelligence, groups often tend to make better decisions than individuals, but this is usually true only when the group has a high level of trust and healthy group dynamics. When they do not, the outcome can be what someone termed "collective dumbness"! In addition, research has shown that if we have experienced a negative emotion, like anger, close in time to when we are making a decision, that emotion may influence our approach to the decision even though the two were unrelated. (If you want to read more on this, consider *Harvard Business Review's* article "Don't Let Emotions Screw Up Your Decisions" by Francesca Gino). Remember, we are complex people. There is nothing simple about human behavior!

8. Spiritualizing decisions.

One of the tempting ways for Christian leaders to respond to confusion and complexity is to spiritualize the problem or decision. You sometimes see this at work when you hear others use such phrases as "God wants us to..." or "We have not prayed enough about this." While all decisions have a spiritual aspect, spiritualization often occurs when a sound decision-making process is eliminated. Spiritualization takes a variety of forms including inappropriately placing God's approval on a decision, confusing prayer with decision-making, and labeling others as nonspiritual when they do not see a situation the same way. However, spiritualization artificially simplifies challenges and seldom leads to wise decisions. Ultimately, it abuses and trivializes God and His Word.

9. Failing to correct a bad decision.

One hard decision for any leader is knowing who to hire. I believe it's fair to say that almost every leader I have ever met (including myself!) has told me stories about mistakes in hiring decisions. One leader was two days away from hiring someone, but after some discussion with one of our consultants as well as some reflection, he realized this was not the right person to hire. At that moment, some leaders would justify moving forward since it is embarrassing to make a correction. But this leader was courageous and told his people, his board, and his candidate that the hire was not going to happen. More often than not, when we feel like we may have made a bad decision, we still continue moving ahead instead of correcting the decision. This not only includes hiring decisions but also other areas of life including dating, marriage, drugs, pornography, finances, and debt.

"Wherever you see a successful business, someone once made a courageous decision." –Peter Drucker

10. Succumbing to decision overload.

The average person today is being confronted with an ever-increasing amount of responsibility and information (aka information overload). Today, the typical adult is faced with:

- Understanding and managing 401(k)/403(b) retirement investments
- Complex medical insurance plans
- Ever-changing computer software
- Technology that is changing about every one or two years
- Overwhelming amount of information from T.V., social media, web-browsing, and print
- Jobs that are often uncertain due consolidation and a rapidly changing economy

Each of the above adds to the number of decisions that need to be made, and the volume of information to process also makes those decisions more complicated. In his book *Paradox of Choice* (2016), Dr. Barry Schwartz notes that while freedom to choose is a good thing, too many options can incapacitate a person's ability to make a decision. Another factor adding to the challenge is what economist Fred Hirsch refers to as the "tyranny of small decisions" – when a person decides to look at one more option, read one more article, go to one more website, etc. This produces even more options, and with too many options, people are inclined to choose none or impulsively choose poorly.

THE 10 DECISION TRAPS

01 Holding too high of an opinion of you.

02 Failing to seek or listen to wise counsel.

03 Making decisions impulsively.

04 Allowing the search for a perfect decision to create paralysis.

05 Facing a decision that exceeds the capacity of the leadership.

06 Viewing questions as an enemy rather than a friend.

07 Failing to understand and manage human dynamics.

08 Spiritualizing decisions.

09 Failing to correct a bad decision.

10 Succumbing to decision overload.

Making Wise Decisions

by Jay Desko, Ph.D.

The Challenges and Consequences

"If any of you lacks wisdom, you should ask God, who gives generously to all without finding fault, and it will be given to you." –James 1:5

When Walt Disney was launching his first business, he borrowed $500 from his uncle. His uncle wanted to be paid back in cash, not in ownership of the new business. If his uncle had decided for repayment with ownership instead of cash, the initial investment would have been worth about $1 billion dollars today! (Source: *The Disney Way*, Bill Capodagli and Lynn Jackson)

How is that for a bad decision!

We have all experienced the consequences of bad decisions, and we have all made at least a few of them! For example...

- **Bad business decisions:** AOL buys Time Warner for $182 billion dollars (yes, BILLIONS) and ends up selling it for $36 billion. A loss of $183 billion dollars when adjusted for inflation!

- **Bad personal life decisions:** A woman who is so hungry to be married that she does not listen to family and friends and marries a guy who ends up cheating on her and ultimately abandoning her after they had a child together!

- **Bad financial decisions:** A young man with student loans decides to quit his job and open up a pizza franchise without even asking for input from his financial advisor or family!

- **Bad hiring decisions:** A leader of a nonprofit organization becomes infatuated with a job candidate and fails to do enough reference checking. If he had, he would have learned that this candidate has had some questionable issues in his past!

- **Bad church leadership decisions:** A church was in a state of conflict and decline for over ten years, but the leadership never sought help and made decisions that made matters even worse!

No organization or leader makes perfect decisions all the time. But during critical points, one bad decision can cause catastrophic failure. Some decisions are a lot easier to make than others. For example, most decisions fall on a continuum of simple to complex. A simple decision is one that requires minimal time and input and the potential risk or consequences of the decision is low. A complex decision requires more time and input and the risks or consequences of the decision are significant.

HOW DECISIONS ARE MADE

For example, a simple decision looks something like this: you are driving with your family and need to decide between Chick-fil-A or Arby's. It's a fast food meal that will last ten minutes. Is it really that hard?!

A more moderate decision may look like this: you are shopping for a car and need to decide between two brands you like and three different models. Your final decision may or may not result in satisfaction with the brand, model, color, price, or options you selected, but in the end, it is not usually going to result in a catastrophic outcome either way.

Complex decisions are different. Here's an example: You are leading a growing church that is running out of space. You need to decide whether to start a new site in a different location, plant a church, or expand your facilities. This is a complex decision since it has far-reaching and long-term consequences.

A common challenge for us as individuals, leaders, and boards is to look at a complex decision as simple or make a simple decision too complex. Making a simple decision too complex adds unnecessary time and bureaucracy and can create frustration among those around us. Making a complex decision too simple can result in impulsive choices, missed input, and bad outcomes.

When Solomon became king of Israel almost 3,000 years ago, he was young, inexperienced, and lacking confidence. Yet, he was smart enough and humble enough to ask God for the ability to discern and make wise decisions.

> "Now, O LORD my God, you have made your servant king in place of my father David. But I am only a little child and do not know how to carry out my duties. Your servant is here among the people you have chosen, a great people, too numerous to count or number. So give your servant a discerning heart to govern your people and to distinguish between right and wrong."
> –1 Kings 3:7-9

Even though Solomon was humble enough to ask for wisdom and even though he experienced extraordinary success, he also made some pretty foolish choices including marrying 700 wives and having another 300 female "partners." Many of these women brought with them beliefs and values very different from those that God expected from Solomon. The result was a dysfunctional family with a lot of detrimental outcomes! Want to make better decisions? If you follow these steps, you will!

1. Decide How to Decide

WHO gets to decide?

With our clients who are facing major decisions, we first discuss how they will make the decision. One key aspect of this is defining WHO has the authority to make this decision. Consider the following groups in relation to decision-making. In each case, it must be decided WHO has the authority to decide. The more you clarify the WHO, the more you reduce the likelihood of conflict.

PRIVATELY HELD BUSINESS	NON-PROFIT	CHURCH
The owner?	The CEO/Director?	The pastor?
A manager?	A manager?	A staff member?
The board?	The board?	The board?
		Church members?

"It is hard to imagine a more stupid or more dangerous way of making decisions than by putting those decisions in the hands of people who pay no price for being wrong." –Thomas Sowell

HOW will the decision be made?

There are generally four approaches regarding how a decision will be made. Whichever approach is chosen is usually influenced by the nature of the decision, the rules or by-laws of the organization, the history and culture of the organization, and the credibility of the leader(s).

- **Decision by an individual** – This may be an owner, manager, or staff member.
- **Decision by a small group** – This is most often a work team, management team, or board.
- **Decision by unanimous consent** – This is when more than one person is involved in the decision and either they want agreement or the by-laws require it.
- **Decision by popular majority** – This is when you must have either a simple majority of 51% or more or a supermajority such as two thirds or three quarters.

Warning: The dangers of unanimous consent

There is something energizing about having everyone affirm a particular decision. It makes us feel more confident in the decision. Some people even take unanimous agreement as a sign of God's affirmation of the decision (in some cases this is a sign of spiritualization). However, while having complete support is a worthy goal, it is not smart to require it in order to move forward with a decision. By requiring complete agreement, one person now has all the power, since it only takes one person to say no, rendering the opinions of all the others as irrelevant. Unanimous consent is really decision-making by one. Desiring unanimous consent is admirable. Requiring it is unwise.

2. Create the Environment

To make a wise decision, you need to first ensure that you have created the right environment for wise decision-making. The six elements needed for a good decision-making environment are expertise, prayer, candor, listening, inquiry, and creativity. Once you have implemented the six core areas, you are ready to discern your options and make your decision. The following decision-making chart shows the elements and flow of making a wise decision. This chart can serve as a valuable tool for you and your group.

1. DECISION-MAKING ENVIRONMENT
EXPERTISE: Inviting the right knowledge and experience to the discussion. *Do we have the expertise?*
PRAYER: Inviting God to guide, shape, and protect. *Have we been seeking God's wisdom?*
CANDOR: Inviting the right knowledge and experience to the discussion. *Have the key voices been heard?*
LISTENING: Respecting what God and others are saying. *Are we open to all ideas?*
INQUIRY: Asking questions to gain clarity and add value. *Have we tested assumptions?*
CREATIVITY: Inviting creative thinkers and encouraging the free flow of ideas. *Have we considered alternatives?*

2. DISCERNING: Evaluating your options		
OPTION 1	OPTION 2	OPTION 3

3. DECIDING: Finalizing the option(s) to pursue	
PROS	CONS
Our decision is...	

4. EXECUTION: Implementing your decision		
STEP 1	STEP 2	STEP 3

3. Make the Decision

If you have created the right environment for making a decision and have evaluated your options, you still must ultimately choose. Sometimes this is tough since you may be choosing between somewhat equally good or difficult options. There are seldom risk free decisions or guarantees. But as leaders, we are responsible to ensure decisions are made. So trust God, trust your team, and make a decision!

"I found every single successful person I've ever spoken to had a turning point. The turning point was when they made a clear, specific unequivocal decision that they were going to achieve success. Some people make that decision at 15 and some people make it at 50, and most people never make it at all." –Brian Tracy

4. Implement the Decision

It is one thing to make a decision; it is a totally different thing to actually implement it. Implementing decisions takes time and planning. It requires accountability, and it is highly likely someone will not like the decision. Since most of us do not embrace conflict (someone who does might just be a bit of a masochist!), we often will start to back away from a decision or shift the blame to someone else if tension begins to rise. I remember one leader referring to a director of a nonprofit organization as "Teflon" because "nothing ever sticks to him!"

"A good decision executed quickly beats a brilliant decision implemented slowly." –Paul Rogers and Marcia Blenko, ***Who Has the D?***

Sometimes, it is wise to back away since the decision may not have been well thought out or the timing may have been bad. However, there are times when the decision is a reasonably wise one and there will never be a "good time." In this case, the leader has to manifest both courage and stamina. If a leader cannot do this, he is a weak leader and will develop a pattern of risk avoidance and coasting, causing great damage over time to the organization and to those around him.

5. Evaluate the Decision

Evaluation is critical after implementing a decision. Use the following checklist to test the quality of your decision. Based on your answers, you will be able to tell if the decision is successful, or if not, where you can improve for next time.

6 Tests for Quality Decision-Making

1. Was a decision made? (status)
2. What was the decision? (content)
3. How was the decision made? (process)
4. How good was the decision? (quality)
5. Was the decision executed? (implementation)
6. Was the decision accepted? (ownership)

"Whatever course you decide upon, there is always someone to tell you that you are wrong. There are always difficulties arising which tempt you to believe that your critics are right. To map out a course of action and follow it to an end requires courage."
–Ralph Waldo Emerson

Take Responsibility for Your Decisions

If you are not courageous enough to take responsibility for a decision, then you are not worthy enough to have the authority to make the decision. Sometimes we like to take credit for the decisions that work well but blame others when the decision fails. Our ability to revise history and self-justify our actions while assigning blame to others for their actions is amazing and dangerously sad! It is the unusual leader who takes responsibility for a decision that is not working by saying, "I am responsible for the decision," or "I am sorry for the decision." These leaders don't blame others. They take responsibility for their actions.

A colleague and I were once having a tense meeting with a client because of a conflict they were having. Due to a decision that we made about who could attend the meeting, the tensions increased before we even started. We immediately took ownership of our decision and apologized for it. At that very moment, the tension left the room, and the client wanted to proceed, demonstrating the power of an apology.

What Next?

Using the decision traps list on page 118, consider the traps that you and your team are most likely to be caught in when making a decision. You may even want to look back on a recent decision that you feel was not successful and use the list of traps to determine why.

Using the decision-making chart on page 125, evaluate and discuss the health of your decision-making environment and what can be done to improve it.

The one responsibility every leader has in common is making decisions. We all have examples of failed decisions in our personal and professional lives, yet we should strive for continued growth in making wise decisions. Such decisions honor God and prevent us from harming people and our organizations. Plus, the alternative to a good decision is a bad option!

“

If you can’t fly then run,
if you can’t run then walk,
if you can’t walk then crawl,
but whatever you do you have
to keep moving forward.

DR. MARTIN LUTHER KING, JR.

Section 4:
How Do We Change?

Implementing & Changing

Smart Change Leadership

by Jay Desko, Ph.D.

Change Is Everywhere

u·biq·ui·tous (yo͞o'bikwədəs). This is one of those difficult-to-pronounce words that make people around the user say, "She must be really smart!" However, the word is a good one to use when describing change. Ubiquitous means "all over the place" or "pervasive." And that describes all the change surrounding us – it's everywhere!

- Change of computer software at work
- Change of medical treatments for disease
- Change of technology in your car
- Change of supervisor at your job
- Change of your health insurance plan
- Change of music styles in your church
- Change of policies at your child's school

Change really is everywhere. One writer in the Bible described it this way in Ecclesiastes 3:

"

There is a time for everything,
and a season for every activity under heaven:

a time to be born and a time to die,
a time to plant and a time to uproot,

a time to kill and a time to heal,
a time to tear down and a time to build,

a time to weep and a time to laugh,
a time to mourn and a time to dance,

a time to scatter stones and a time to gather them,
a time to embrace and a time to refrain,

a time to search and a time to give up,
a time to keep and a time to throw away,

a time to tear and a time to mend,
a time to be silent and a time to speak,

a time to love and a time to hate,
a time for war and a time for peace.

Ecclesiastes 3:1-8

Change can be a bit overwhelming at times and especially frustrating when it is not understood or it is just plain dumb. On more than one occasion, I have heard one of my children describe a change they did not appreciate with these profound words: "That's stupid." It is the responsibility of the smart change leader to lead smart changes in smart ways!

As leaders and managers, changes are not only shaping you, you are shaping change by the way you lead your team, the way you manage communication, and the way you personally respond to change yourself. Change leadership is a vital responsibility for every leader and manager. The title of an interesting book about change shows how important it is: *Change or Die!* This chapter is designed to give you a better understanding of change so you can lead yourself and others more effectively through it and be a smart change leader.

In addition, every time you see this symbol, there is a helpful tool or exercise for you to work through on your own or, more preferably, with your team.

Life Cycle of an Organization

People and organizations have something in common – they both follow a predictable life cycle from birth to decline. While for some, the cycle is short and quick, for others the cycle can play out over many decades. It is helpful for leaders and managers to understand this cycle.

THE LIFE CYCLE OF AN ORGANIZATION

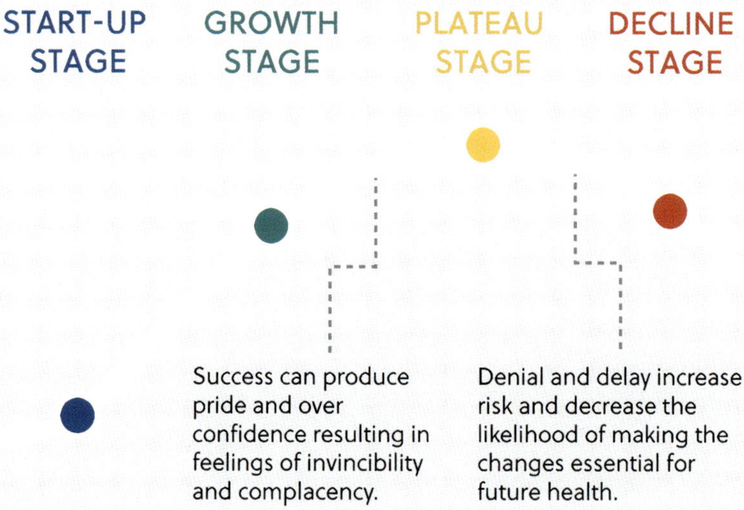

Discuss with your leaders where in the cycle you feel your organization is at this time and why.

Recently, there was news of a nationally known and fast growing organization that went out of existence within six months of experiencing a leadership crisis. People were shocked, articles were written, and social media went wild. Why? Because people were surprised that an organization in a massive growth cycle could ever decline so quickly. But they can, and they do. Sometimes they die because of not changing and other times because the leaders are not wisely managing change. Either way, the result is the same: disillusionment, disappointment, and sometimes even disdain. As Helen Keller once said, “The saddest thing in life is people who can see but have no vision!”

How People Process Change

Everyone processes change differently. For example, some people overall love change and are quick to adapt, while others fear change and are slower to adapt. It is wise to consider not only how you process change, but also how some of your key leaders and constituents process it. By understanding how others process change, you can be better prepared to provide what they need to adapt to the new initiative.

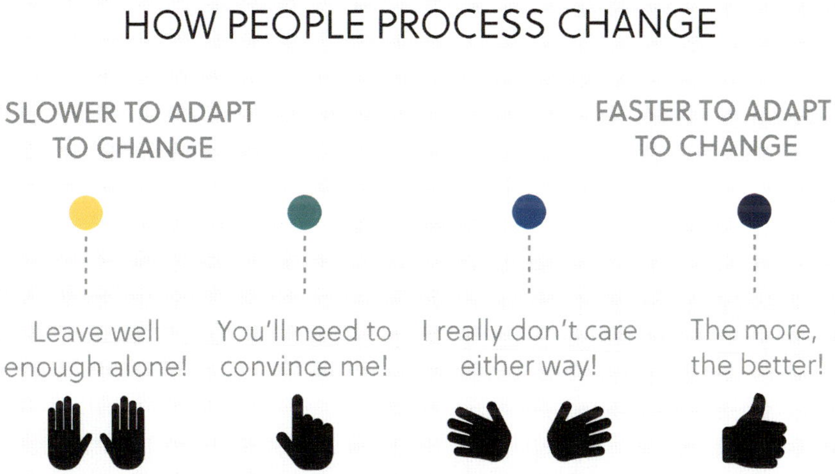

Determine where you and your key leaders fall on the change scale.

Essentials of Smart Change Leadership

Have you ever gone camping? Or prepared for a major storm? If so, you know it is important to be sure to have the "essentials": food, water, and batteries, for example. The same is true for leading change. You increase the likelihood of success by ensuring that you understand and use the three essentials of smart change leadership:

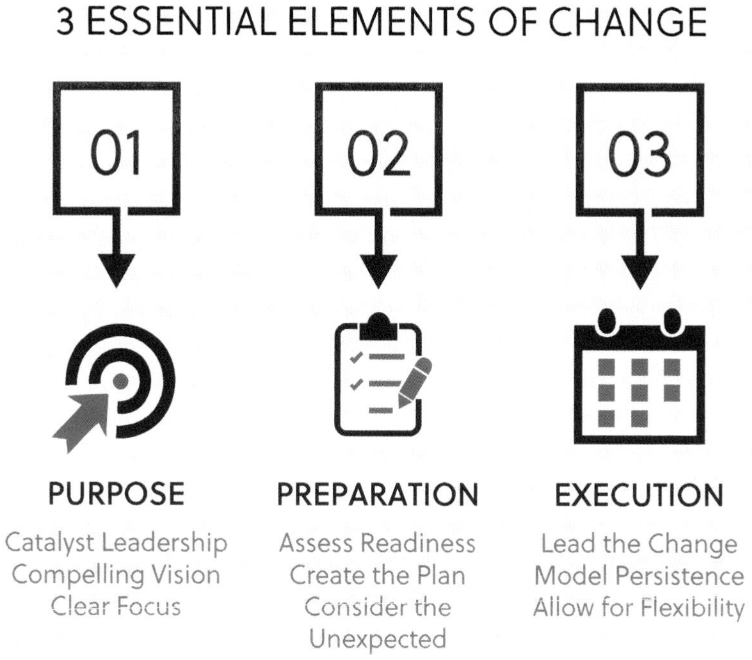

If a change fails, it will be due to something lacking in one of these three essentials. Each of the three essential elements requires successful actions as noted in the graphic above. The following sections will provide you with practical guidance on each of these three essentials.

Purpose

Jack is the pastor of a church of 200 people. But twenty years ago, it was a church of almost 500 and was viewed as healthy, vibrant and innovative. He loved people and was a good care-giver to them. However, he was not a catalyst, and therefore, he seldom could come up with an idea or change that would ignite others toward the church's mission. In addition, because of his cautious personality, he would not embrace the ideas that came from two people who were catalysts – his youth pastor and one of his board members. Because of Jack's lack of compelling purpose, the church will continue to decline, lose people, and experience the loss of the few catalysts he had. Jack's problem was not that he was not a catalyst. After all, not every leader is gifted this way. His problem was that he did not know how to utilize those who were. Smart change leaders are either catalysts for change or surround themselves with those who are.

Catalyst Leadership

What does catalyst leadership look like?

Some may think catalyst leaders are super-human. They are not! They just have a set of talents that God has given them that, when used wisely, can make a big difference. The most effective catalyst leaders are a unique blend of some of the following characteristics. A catalyst leader:

- Is a compelling communicator
- Takes risks
- Inspires others
- Possesses exceptional wisdom
- Maintains a high level of credibility
- Creates meaningful ideas
- Attracts influential followers

Compelling Vision

How do you create a compelling vision?

Every change needs a compelling vision or rationale. The longer, more complex, or muddier it becomes, the less likely the change is to survive. Author John Kotter says that if you can't communicate the vision to someone in five minutes or less and get a reaction that signifies both understanding and interest, you are not done creating it.

Three important steps to creating a compelling vision are to:

1. Explain the problem or opportunity
2. Provide a clear, concise, and compelling solution
3. Share this in a way that reaches the heart of the people, not just the head

(Additional resources that may be helpful are: *Making Vision Stick* by Andy Stanley and *The Heart of Change* by John Kotter.)

What is the role of providing a vision that inspires hope?

As far back as the 1950s, psychologists and psychiatrists were trying to assess which approaches to counseling were most effective. What they discovered was, in general, it did not matter. Many people experienced positive change from the counseling regardless of the therapeutic approach. The common element the researchers discovered connected to the effectiveness was hope. It wasn't the particular model of counseling that inspired the change, but rather, it was the hope that came from the help that was being provided. In applying this principle to the change process, people are more likely to be motivated to change when they experience hope – believing that what comes after the change takes place will be better than the present state. Smart change leaders inspire hope! (For more on this topic, consider reading *Change or Die* by Alan Deutschman.)

Clear Focus

How important is focus?

Cognitive researchers believe most people can only give attention to no more than 4-7 pieces of information at a time. Smart change leaders have the unique ability to keep the organization focused even in the midst of the noises and distractions common to life. Focus is what you see in great athletes and other performers who, even in the midst of 60,000 people, can tune out and zero in. Focus is important in leading change because it is essential to accomplishing the vision to which all change should be connected. Without focus, a leader or manager will drift off target and begin to work on a new idea or get caught up in micro issues rather than vital macro issues. (For additional reading in this area, I recommend Daniel Goleman's book, *Focus*.)

How to work through the stages of idea generation

The following graphic shows a healthy process for generating new ideas and solutions to problems. Sometimes teams or leaders slip into Idea Evaluation too quickly, quenching Idea Generation. Other times, a leader generates too many ideas but doesn't implement them.

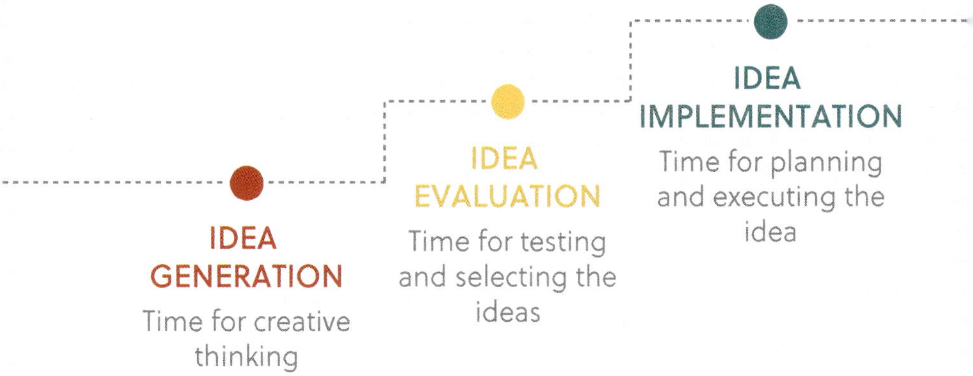

At which of these three stages are you/your team best and weakest?

Preparation

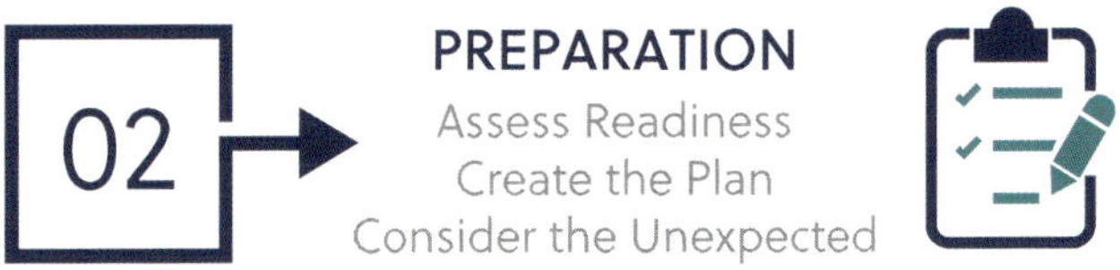

Sharon was a visionary leader of a mid-sized business. She was a catalyst for new ideas and change. While not every one of her ideas was a success, she hit a number of home runs over the years of leading this business. However, at times, Sharon's staff would grow frustrated because she would sometimes generate the idea but not take the time to test it or consider the planning needed for success. Smart change leaders need to not only ensure the creation of new initiatives but also make sure they prepare for them.

Assess Readiness

How to determine if there is a felt need for change

Quite often people deny the realities that are surrounding them, either because they cannot see how serious matters are or they fear that change may result in a personal loss to them. Four of the most common signs that an organization is not interested in or ready for change are:

- Things do not seem all that bad
- There is evidence that all is not well but these signs are ignored
- There is a resistance to anyone who may provide data for change

- There is a sense of forced optimism where people are expected to talk positively

In his book *Necessary Endings*, Dr. Henry Cloud talks about moments of truth when we have to decide to embrace a change or to embrace "average."

> "The pruning moment is that clarity of enlightenment when we become responsible for making the decision to either own the vision or not. If we own it, we have to prune. If we don't, we have decided to own the other vision, the one we called average. It is a moment of truth that we encounter almost every day in many, many decisions." –Henry Cloud, *Necessary Endings*, 2011

How does this quote possibly relate to the circumstances you are presently facing in your personal life or organization?

How to assess the leadership credibility before launching change

Change requires leadership capital. In other words, you will need enough credibility in the bank before you can succeed in influencing others to follow you toward change. A major change usually requires major credibility reserves, and smaller changes require smaller credibility reserves.

To assess credibility...

1. Identify the people who are most important to the success of your leadership and attempt to assess how much credibility you have with them.

2. Seek feedback from other mature leaders regarding their perception of your credibility.

3. What behaviors, decisions and actions have cost you the most credibility? Were they worth it?

4. What upcoming changes will require significant credibility? Do you have enough credibility to succeed in this change?

5. What should you begin doing to improve credibility?

Credibility Builders

- Always acting with integrity
- Continually improving your skills
- Doing what you say you will do
- Admiting mistakes and correcting them
- Solving problems
- Listening to suggestions and feedback
- Sharing information openly and freely
- Being accessible and visible

Credibility

Credibility Destroyers

- Behaving unethically or immorally
- Lacking pursuit of relationships
- Lacking follow through
- Not returning calls and emails
- Sharing inaccurate information
- Lacking honesty and transparency
- Being unwilling to listen to others
- Failing to admit and correct mistakes

Create the Plan

How do you implement the change you are making?

1. Define the goals necessary for accomplishing the new initiative
2. Determine who will lead each goal
3. Create a path for implementation including dates for action and communication
4. Incorporate ongoing accountability
5. Conduct ongoing evaluation and adjust as needed

Remember: Change will often take much LONGER than you plan and seldom unfold the way you expect.

Consider the Unexpected

Have you considered the unexpected? Unexpected things can emerge at the most inconvenient time! Leaders need to consider some of these by doing scenario planning. While it is not possible to consider or plan for every unexpected thing that can happen, the following graphic will help you plan for some of the events that can happen to you.

What happens if...?

PERSONNEL
Moral failure
Medical crisis
Key leader quits/terminated

FINANCIAL
Key donor(s) stops giving
Economic crisis
Momentum slows

POLITICAL
Change of board
Change of catalyst leadership

Execution

Mike was the director of a small nonprofit. The leadership team of this organization loved working together. They would hold planning retreats and discuss new ideas that would address weaknesses in the organization and serve its constituents more effectively. But more often than not, nothing ever happened. They talked, and talked, and talked, and yet there was seldom any follow through. As the leader, Mike contributed to this culture of "all talk, no execution" by not providing an implementation plan or accountability. Smart change leaders know how to move from vision to action!

Lead the Change

How to understand and manage resistance to change

Resistance to change is normal. Change is inconvenient, makes people feel a bit confused and embarrassed, and can often result in a sense of loss. Remember, not everyone who resists a change is an obstructionist. Sometimes they resist it because either they don't understand it or they see a problem with it. After all, people fight to protect what they value! The following graphic will help you better understand and manage resistance.

Where are you already or most likely going to experience resistance to the change you are considering? What will you do to better understand why they are resisting? What will you do to manage this resistance?

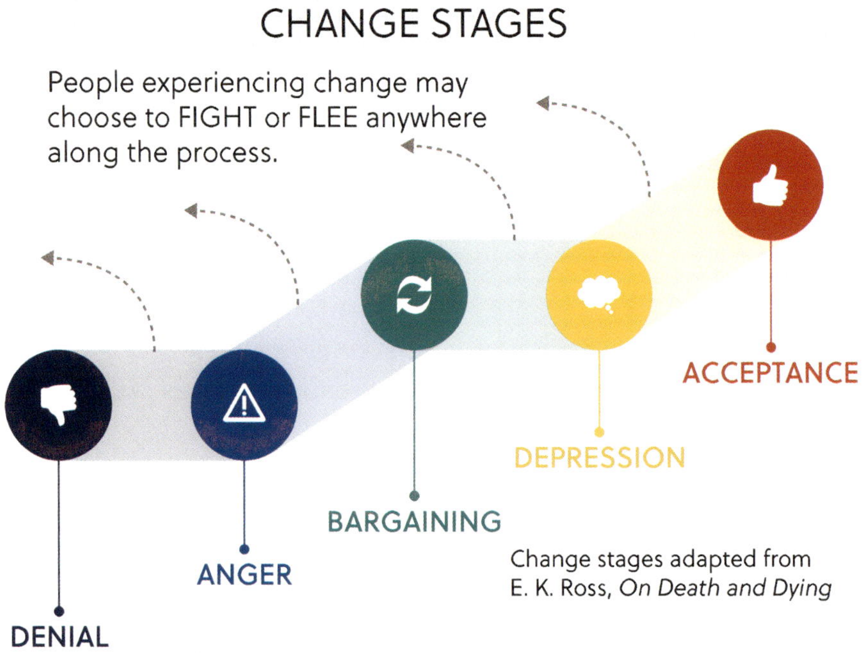

What are the top four implementation killers?

1. Failure to cut through organizational obstacles
2. Failure to assign a person to own it or a completion date
3. Failure to empower people to implement
4. Failure to hold people accountable

Which implementation killers are most common in your organization? How will you reduce them?

What mistakes can turn smart change leadership into dumb change leadership?

1. Failing to seek or listen to counsel
2. Having unhealthy team dynamics
3. Lacking a compelling vision for the change

4. Inadequately assessing likely resistance
5. Doing too much too quickly
6. Doing too little too slowly
7. Inadequately communicating about the change
8. Not being transparent about the change
9. Not having enough financial resources
10. Not having enough credibility and trust
11. Not having enough "critical mass" support
12. Implementing the change poorly
13. Quitting too soon – not enough grit!

Model Persistence

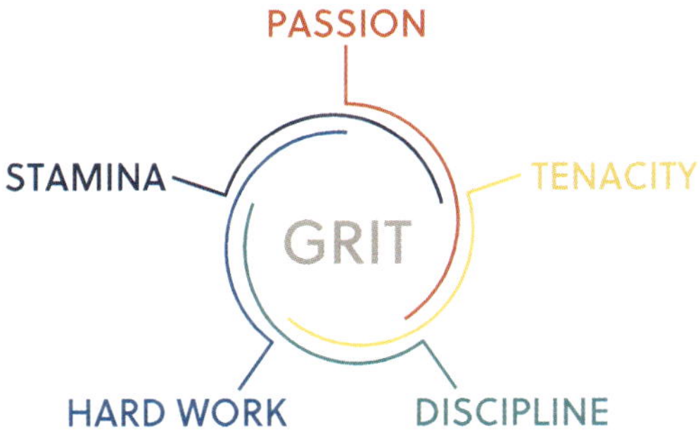

What is grit and what does grit require?
Grit is a term being used by some psychologists to describe the character trait of self-discipline. Grittiness is a common characteristic that sets apart those who are average from those who are exceptional. The following people would most likely have self-discipline as a common characteristic:

- Those who start a business or nonprofit and succeed
- Those who finish college or a training program
- Those who maintain physical fitness

- Those who develop exceptional abilities in music, sports and science
- Those who quit smoking
- Those who excel at sales
- Those who resist unhealthy or impulsive behaviors
- Those who spend less and save more

Self-discipline, which includes hard work, tenacity, passion and stamina, results in a leader who chooses not to quit when circumstances get tough. One biblical writer describes it this way: "Get rid of the things that hinder you and run with perseverance" (Hebrews 12:1-3).

Allow for Flexibility

When handling change, unexpected issues may arise. You as the leader need to be able to calmly handle the surprises that you face and be flexible to find a new solution for your organization. In addition, it is important to not "sell" your vision as being guaranteed or perfect because most change initiatives seldom are. You want to create a learning culture that allows for experimenting. You want to create a culture that is agile and open to modifying direction when evidence arises to demonstrate it would not be best to remain on the original course. There is a different and sometimes even better way.

The success or failure of the changes that you implement will be largely influenced by how well you lead the process. Smart change leaders surround themselves with catalysts and inspire hope. Smart change leaders ensure the creation and preparation of new initiatives. Smart change leaders know how to move from vision to action. Lead smart!

Avoiding Transition Mistakes

by Jay R. Desko, Ph.D.

4 Phases of Transitions

Silver Lake Services, Inc. had a hard time helping its long-time leader retire. It was a little bumpy, and some of the common signs of turbulence associated with the transition of a long tenured key leader were evident: the leader did not want to be told "it was time"; the board was fearful to push him too hard; the leader was uncertain what he would do next in his life; the board was looking forward to seeing what a new leader could do; the leader felt like the organization would struggle without him; and the board was fearful of conflict and related risks. The board made a few key mistakes in managing this transition, but little did they know some of their biggest mistakes would come after the leader had already left. If the transition of the previous leader caused some turbulence, the search, hiring and on-boarding of the new leader resulted in a *major crash*.

The staff transition process creates both exciting opportunity but also significant vulnerability. Transitions can be for any number of reasons including: voluntary retirement, poor performance, voluntary resignation, or ethical misconduct. Each of these reasons has its own unique potential complications, and mistakes can be easily made during the transition process which includes the following phases:

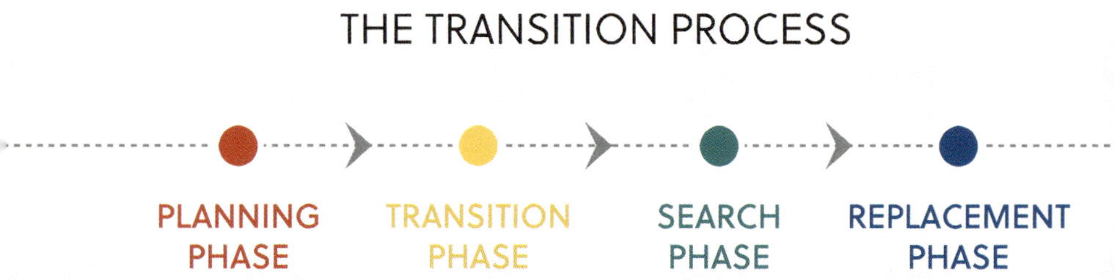

26 Common Errors Made During the Transition Process

The following are 26 common errors we have seen organizations make during the transition process. As consultants, it is our desire to help leaders guard against these errors and thereby increase the likelihood of a successful staffing change.

Mistakes made with your organization, leadership, and remaining staff

1. Assuming you don't have any "hairline cracks" or serious problems to address within the organization.

2. Providing inadequate and infrequent communication to the organization.

3. Allowing the organization to go on a holding pattern during the transition process.

4. Ignoring significant undiscussed issues among the remaining leadership.

5. Having conflict and trust issues within the staff, leadership, or overall organization, but still moving forward with the search.

6. Failing to utilize, pay attention to, communicate with and care for the remaining staff whose knowledge may be helpful and whose anxiety may be heightened.

Mistakes made with the staff member who is leaving

7. Avoiding succession discussion and planning due to fear of conflict with the existing staff member or leader.

8. Allowing the transitioning staff member to have too much influence in the search and hiring process.

9. Allowing a previous leader to stay on staff in a different role without carefully considering the risks with the new leader.

10. Failing to “finish well” with the existing staff member including agreed upon expectations of behavior.

Mistakes made in planning

11. Launching a search process prematurely.

12. Assuming you can conduct a search the way you did the last time, which for some positions may have been 20-30 years ago.

13. Failing to develop a clear, compelling and unifying sense of vision and priorities before making the new hire.

14. Failing to develop an agreed upon profile for the next successful candidate.

15. Creating cumbersome steps in the process such as a lengthy application.

Mistakes made in transition

16. Using an interim leader who has aspirations to be the next leader.

17. Using an interim or temp person to fill a position without clearly managing the expectations.

Mistakes made with the search team

18. Failing to acquire legal counsel at critical points in the transition and hiring process.

19. Having inadequate skills and experience resident within the leadership or staff to conduct a successful recruitment process.

20. Developing "search fatigue" that results in prematurely hiring a candidate who may not be the best choice.

Mistakes made in choosing the candidate

21. Looking for a candidate who is an "A" in every category including leader, speaker, relater, and visionary.

22. Underestimating the importance of a candidate's spouse in senior level leadership positions.

23. Failing to conduct adequate background and reference checks.

24. Failing to adequately assess the candidate for fit with the organization, leadership and staff.

25. Spiritualizing your decisions by claiming, "This is God's person for us."

26. Failing to realize a mistake in the hiring process will cost you a lot of money and pain, often reaching $150,000-$250,000.

Questions to Ask Before Moving Forward

Each question may not be applicable to every staff transition, but at least one question or more should be applicable to your unique context.

1. Consider the four phases below. Can you recall a time in a previous staff transition where one or more of these phases were missed or mismanaged?

In some cases, you will not have much, if any, of a planning phase since a person may have unexpectedly quit, experienced a life-threatening illness, or had a moral event disqualify him or her. It is important to discuss how you would deal with the unexpected vacancy before it happens, especially in key leadership positions.

2. As noted below, you usually have three options when dealing with a staff member who is not performing at the level needed or can no longer do the present role. Which do you feel is the wisest choice in light of your knowledge of the context?

Repair – help the person to be more successful in the role by way of training, coaching and providing reasonable accommodations.

Reposition – move the person into a different role that will be a better fit for his or her skills. This is especially worth considering when the person is well liked and a good fit for the organization's culture.

Replace – transition the person out of the organization.

3. Will the staff member be considered for a different or modified role? If, so, what are the risks and rewards for this and for the person who replaces the staff member?

4. Will you consider an internal candidate? If so, what type of assessment and coaching are you presently using to determine the credibility and competency of existing staff?

5. If the staff member is leaving due to retirement, what is the expectation you have regarding his or her future relationship with the organization? Has this been discussed with him or her?

Staff transitions are one of the more risky times for an organization and often can have unintended effects. We encourage you to seek counsel and think carefully as you work through such staffing changes. When done well, such transitions provide an opportunity for new ideas, new relationships and new momentum. When done poorly, they can result in relational conflict, financial loss, and decline of organizational health and effectiveness.

Crisis Management

by Jay R. Desko, Ph.D.

10 Tips for Managing a Crisis

Unexpected things happen. An employee embezzles funds. A disgruntled staff member attacks another member. A volunteer sexually assaults a constituent. Such crises can threaten the operations, reputation and overall health and well-being of the organization. While the crisis itself is damaging enough, it can get worse when managed unwisely. The following are ten tips for managing an organizational crisis.

1. Act!

Be quick and decisive. To ignore what is emerging or delay in taking action will only allow the situation to worsen. It is much less difficult when you do not let the crisis get too far ahead of you. If the crisis poses a threat to public safety, the primary concern should be to act quickly to ensure the safety of others. Failure to do so will increase the damage from the crisis.

2. Learn.

Don't jump to conclusions prematurely. Gather the facts before making statements and major decisions. Premature decisions or incomplete information can result in making the crisis worse.

3. Seek guidance.

It is often valuable to seek legal, organizational and public relations counsel early on in managing the crisis.

4. Inform.

Depending on the nature of your organization and the crisis, it is wise to inform those above you regarding what is taking place. This may be a supervisor, board, insurance carrier or legal authorities.

5. Be visible.

Demonstrate that someone is in charge and working to make things better. A visible leader will calm the natural uncertainty and anxiety that arise during such critical events.

6. Put people first.

In a crisis, leaders will sometimes adopt a "cover yourself" or "cover the organization" attitude. Don't allow utilitarianism to prevail by placing personal or organizational interests first. Put people first. Depending upon the circumstances, it may be those who believe they were harmed or those who were accused.

7. Own it.

If there is something the leader or organization needs to take responsibility for, do it. Apologizing is always the right thing to do even if the crisis was unintentional.

However, some apology strategies are much more effective than others. If you desire to put those affected by the crisis first, take note of the following four practices when apologizing.

1. Don't attack the accuser.
2. Don't blame others for the crisis.
3. Don't deny that the crisis happened.
4. Don't make excuses for why the crisis happened.

Taking responsibility and offering a sincere apology goes a long way in healing.

8. Communicate liberally and consistently.

Designate a primary communicator. The best way to prevent or minimize rumors is to share as many of the facts as possible. Make sure what you share is accurate and consistent. When mistakes are made, they must be corrected, but that will also make the organization look incompetent. Be honest about what you know and what you don't know, and don't speculate.

9. Document everything.

Keep a file of notes and documentation to help you acquire clear understanding and make wise decisions. Such a file should be kept in a secure place since it will contain very confidential information.

10. Declare an end.

Some organizations perpetuate a crisis by continuing to make it the focal point for too long of a period of time. Remember, the crisis is not the mission. It is important to officially declare an end to the crisis (but not prematurely) and once again share the compelling vision for the future.

10 STEPS FOR MANAGING A CRISIS

01 Act!

02 Learn.

03 Seek guidance.

04 Inform.

05 Be visible.

06 Put people first.

07 Own it.

08 Communicate liberally and consistently.

09 Document everything.

10 Declare an end.

We hope this book has helped you to navigate the challenges that come with leadership. Don't hesitate to contact The Center if we can be of further assistance to you on your journey to lead well!

Who We Are

We are 100% focused on leaders.

With Christian values as our organization's foundation, our mission is to help leaders in businesses, nonprofits and churches lead well.

We make you our first priority.

We have nothing to gain by "selling" you services you don't need.

We customize our services for you.

Our team of experienced consultants and staff customizes services for you and your organization's needs.

We listen and learn to help you lead.

We make sure we fully understand your unique context, vision, and needs before we recommend the services we believe will provide the solutions for your needs.

We build long-lasting relational connections.

We stay connected to many of our clients long after the contract has ended. In fact, many of our clients have contracted with us multiple times over many years.

We not only provide solutions, we help you implement them.

Our consultants work with you and your other leaders by providing ongoing coaching, encouragement, and accountability to increase your success.

Our Solutions

- Executive Coaching
- Leader and Staffing Assessment
- Leadership Development
- Marketing and Communication Advising
- Succession Planning
- Crisis Guidance
- Action Planning
- Staffing Guidance
- H.R. Guidance
- Personalized Coaching Retreats
- Board/Owner Advising
- Organizational Structure Design
- New Market Assessment and Development
- Merger Acquisition Guidance and Coaching

Fees

The Center is a nonprofit organization. Our fees are determined by the services you request and your ability to pay. Don't let fees prevent you from contacting us. We will do all we can to find a workable solution for you.

Contact Us

To learn more about how our team can assist you, please contact us at **215-723-2325** or visit our website, **www.centerconsulting.org**.

Assessment Tools

Leader 360° Process

This process includes gathering anonymous perspectives of how your leadership is viewed by you, your supervisor(s), your peers, and those who report to you. Such feedback is one of the most accurate ways to identify strengths, areas of improvement, and possible blind spots.

Pre-Hire 360°

The Pre-Hire 360 is designed to assist you in acquiring feedback on a candidate from three categories: personal, professional, and self. This report will provide you with insight into your critical hiring decisions.

Personality Testing

Our personality assessments provide a variety of insights into an individual's behaviors, motivators, strengths, areas of development, traditional personality traits, and job-centered behavioral characteristics. They can be used for both pre-hire screening and coaching an employee or team of employees.

Employee Performance Review

Our easy and accurate web-based process collects and computes feedback between the employee and his or her manager to encourage meaningful feedback. This process promotes a fair and open discussion about how to maximize the strengths of each team member.

Group Assessments

Board Assessment: Includes a survey and/or confidential phone interviews of board members to identify strengths, perceptions, and areas of improvement.

Employee Satisfaction Survey: Includes a survey of your employees to identify perceptions regarding job satisfaction, benefits, morale, and other themes.

Organizational Health Assessment

This assessment includes our custom-designed surveys, confidential interviews, and facilitated discussions about your organizational health and the relational health of your team to give you objectivity and foresight in making wise decisions.